BENEATH
THE
BALANCE

The Quiet Revolution of Stability
in a World Obsessed with Balance

BY DR. REGAN OSBORNE

First published by Busybird Publishing 2026

ISBN:
Print: 978-1-923501-65-2
Ebook: 978-1-923501-66-9

The information in this book is based on the author's experiences and opinions. The author and publisher disclaim responsibility for any adverse consequences that may result from use of the information contained herein. Permission to use any external content has been sought by the author. Any breaches will be rectified in further editions of the book.

Cover Image: Dr. Regan Osborne

Cover design: Dr. Regan Osborne

Layout and typesetting: Busybird Publishing

Busybird Publishing
2/118 Para Road
Montmorency, Victoria
Australia 3094

www.busybird.com.au

Author's Note on Collaboration

This work has been written and authored entirely by Dr. Regan Osborne. Throughout the development of Beneath the Balance, I engaged the assistance of AI as an editorial and research tool to help refine structure and to assist in sourcing references. Whilst this technology supported the refinement of ideas, all concepts, interpretations, and philosophical positions expressed within these pages are my own. The insights, perspectives, and conclusions presented herein originate from my personal study, professional experience, and creative reflection.

Contents

'*... nothing in the world is harder than convincing someone of an unfamiliar truth.*'

Patrick Rothfuss, *The Wise Man's Fear*

N.B. Please keep your heart and mind open through this book, but hold a large grain of salt on your tongue. I have written it with a very large grain on mine. This book is a philosophical exploration of a matter that will continue to evolve and change over the years to come. So do not take offence too readily, and please understand that my heart is to see chiropractic, art and philosophy, not just succeed in the world to come, but flourish beyond our wildest comprehension.

For those of us who want to contribute to shaping mankind's evolution, language is where we start.

Preface

'We think in language. The quality of our thoughts and ideas can only be as good as the quality of our language.'

- George Carlin -

To move forward as a profession and a larger industry, chiropractic and the health sciences must understand how our history has brought us, our language, and our practice to its current paradigm and limitations. As philosopher George Santayana famously cautioned: 'Those who cannot remember the past are condemned to repeat it.'

For those who have little experience or knowledge of chiropractic and its history, let me provide a quick preface, at least to what's relevant for this book. Chiropractic stands uniquely among healthcare disciplines as perhaps the closest to being genuinely structural and physically restorative in its interventions. Chiropractors primarily address subluxations:

Essentially, a vertebral subluxation occurs when the joints of the spine fail to move properly, causing interference with the nerve messages from the brain to the body and/or from the body to the brain. This can affect movement patterns, muscle balance and even the function of organs and the chemicals and hormones they produce. Most subluxations do not cause pain (as the majority of nerves are not nociceptive or pain-sensing).

New Zealand Chiropractors' Association (NZCA)

Historically, chiropractors have been sharply divided into two principal groups: the vitalists and the mechanists. The vitalists are the originals, the torchbearers of the ideas on which the profession was built. They are philosophically based on holistic care that seeks to nurture and facilitate healing throughout the entire system. They operate from a beautiful faith in the awe-inspiring power of the human body and the power that made it. Vitalists are happy to play and explore the unknown. Conversely, mechanists ground themselves firmly in evidence-based caution. They see and give credence to the vast quantities of unknowns that remain in the practice of chiropractic. Their perspective prioritises measurable outcomes, precision, and risk aversion. Where outcomes can be clearly predicted, they act decisively; where uncertainty reigns, they prefer restraint. Both philosophies hold significant merit and relevance, yet their friction has been one of the most significant factors contributing to our professional rigidity.

Few chiropractors dispute that the physical applications of our principles have changed little since the 1950s. In fact, it would be fair to be so blunt as to say that we have stagnated, sitting on the laurels of the incredible minds that came before us, unsure of where or how to proceed. Although we have refined many techniques, developed new ways of quantifying our work, and have been quick to employ new technologies, the frameworks of and approaches to our skeletal corrections have changed little. A principal reason for this stagnation is a pervasive culture of self-censorship driven by statements like: *'We're all doing the same thing, just differently.'* This self-imposed conformity stifles innovation and evolution, but also unites us to stand against a long history of external suppression and ridicule.

> *'Great spirits have always encountered violent opposition from mediocre minds.'*
>
> **- Albert Einstein -**

From the early 1900s through the late 1980s, the chiropractic profession endured severe persecution, notably spearheaded by the American Medical Association (AMA). Formed as a trade union rather than a scientific body, it monopolised research, dictated educational content, and aggressively manipulated public perception through its sponsored media partners to drive business for its members. Chiropractors were systematically defamed, legally challenged, and unjustly imprisoned. Ironically, when the defamation started, there were no quality control or scientific standards beyond the amount paid to the AMA. This means that at the time, the 'research' for their own interventions was just as, if not more, flaccid than that for chiropractic.

Eventually, to defeat this goliath, chiropractors put aside their petty in-house squabbles between universities or techniques and joined together to sue the AMA for defamation. Eventually, the chiropractic community courageously fought back, securing a groundbreaking legal victory against the AMA for defamation in 1987. The battle was won, but the war between 'healing in a bottle' and 'healing from within' was just beginning.

Part of the longer-lasting effects of this time in our history came from the decisions that were made to unite our profession. We developed unspoken rules to bring us together. One of our most damaging unwritten laws came from this: no discussion or challenging of another technique or method at professional gatherings. Part of the reasoning for this development lay also in the veracity and passion with which practitioners would argue and pick at each other's techniques and methods. Given the high tensions and stakes at this time, this is not a huge surprise; we're a passionate group. However, this unwritten law has done almost as much damage to the exploration and furthering of chiropractic as the 'we are all doing the same thing, just differently' catchphrase. Quick as a flash, our profession's exploration and evolution of the physical applications of our knowledge and philosophy ground to a screeching halt.

Here in this little ecosystem, we see the effects of self-censorship on a community at a larger scale displayed in full colour over a generous expanse of time. Techniques remain unchallenged and thus unchanged, creating a protected inner circle and an implicit orthodoxy within chiropractic education and practice. Our universities, designed to foster innovation, became custodians of tradition, reinforcing a culture resistant to genuine inquiry and experimentation. Techniques are passed down like sacred rites, insulated from scrutiny and guarded by loyalty more so than results. Thus, the chiropractic industry now begins to resemble the gargantuan monstrosity of its pharmaceutical antagonist more than the grassroots hero that its humble beginnings intended. The majority of our representative bodies, and even a large part of our cohort, could now be diagnosed with a form of Stockholm Syndrome or cognitive dissonance as they seek acceptance and validation from the same people who have repressed and bullied them.

This no-go zone in our profession led to a renaissance in the 1960s and 1970s into the understanding and utilisation of energetic techniques by brilliant doctors such as George Goodheart, Donny Epstein, Victor Frank, and Scott Walker. These creative genius souls and their works were a natural response to the limitations in place around the physical applications of chiropractic. Exploring new ways of treating the body physically was, at the very least, subconsciously off-limits to the creatives of this era. Instead, the creativity flowed into the path of least resistance: energetics and emotions. For this, I am eternally grateful.

My journey into this discourse comes as a second-generation chiropractor. My father, Dr. Stephen Osborne, is a world-class vitalistic practitioner who has zealously pursued a thorough understanding of techniques related to almost every avenue of intervention: osseous, muscular, fascial, emotional, energetic, naturopathic, homeopathic and visceral. Indeed, it was inevitable that my brother, wife, and I all eventually joined the chiropractic ranks. When you spend time around someone as passionate as my dad, it's difficult to not become inspired.

I was preparing to graduate from university, loaded with as much knowledge and information as was useful from my classes, and with as much passion, expertise and practical knowledge I could absorb from my father and the many other practitioners I had spent time observing. I was doing a final year placement in Dr. Mark Postle's clinic on the Sunshine Coast when I stumbled into an experience that would change my world forever and set me on this journey: I was offered the opportunity to experience a new technique they had been implementing in the clinic.

I was there for four weeks, and in that time, my whole body changed significantly. I could breathe better, run better (ending my 13-year relationship with Foot Levelers orthotics), sing better, and stand taller and easier. It wasn't just an improvement in one part of my body or how

I perceived it: every aspect of my body improved simultaneously. As someone who had received regular chiropractic care, kinesiology, and personal training for rehab, it perplexed me. If chiropractic really had been doing everything I thought and it claimed it was, how was this improvement possible?

'To honour our tradition is not to preserve it unchanged, but to deepen it through scrutiny.'

- Rupert Sheldrake -

As Sheldrake suggests, true science is not a fixed dogma, but a method of perpetual inquiry. To stop asking is to stop evolving.

Introduction

Language is both the clay and the potter of our society. The art and the artist. 'It is from the heart the mouth speaks' (Luke 6:45 NKJV), suggesting that language can illuminate not just what is at the depths of our being, but also what we desire and long for in those depths. Speaking those desires is what makes their achievement possible; it brings energy and intention into the world to begin the fruition process.

When we name a thing, we can know it and understand it. Naming is a crucial step in healing: along with the 'desire to heal', it provides the spark of revelation, the launching pad of exploration and contemplation. Neuroscientific research underscores this transformative power through 'affect labelling', which reveals that naming an emotion directly quiets the brain's reactive circuits, fostering internal coherence and calming turbulent states (Lieberman et al., 2007). Sometimes the name is whispered gently, sometimes it comes as painfully as a blunt razor pulled against soft skin. Occasionally, naming defies clarity for years, cloaked in ambiguity and concealed beneath well-intentioned protocols and fragmented methodologies. Without this mindful inquiry, we remain like fish trapped in shallow tide pools, endlessly debating puddle clarity, oblivious to the vast truths of the ocean lying just beyond our immediate vision.

Much of our Western culture is obsessed with a very shallow band of names: labels such as titles, genders, diagnoses, and pronouns. Whilst frequently misinformed and shortsighted, this does point to a more profound truth: our words and language **are** critical. Over the last century, we have been encouraged to wield our language and words carelessly and without much, if any, considerable thought.

Atheistic-socialistic worldviews are illustrative of this, promoting a flattening of modern existence and subsequently depriving value and meaning from our language and, thus, the individual. This political dogma reduces individuals to convenient categories or disposable economic units. On the other hand, corporate capitalist rhetoric commodifies language until words hollow into empty vessels, so that mere branding, shallow slogans, and impersonal contracts supplant genuine sincerity. Both systematically erase the complexity of the soulful and intelligent being from our discourse — in one we become a number, in the other, a product.

The lack of value in our words is subtly, often unintentionally, reinforced by mottos such as: 'it's all about intent' or 'it's not what you say but how you say it'. Both are true, but not necessarily the whole truth; of course, what you say is also important, regardless of how you say it. However, our language is both the culprit and the victim of modern history. So, we must take heed and caution, contemplating our words and how we use them, regarding them with as much fear and reverence as the awesome first breaths of a newborn babe or the razor edge of a surgeon's scalpel. We must approach language as we approach the body itself: with reverence for its innate intelligence and its astonishing capacity to adapt. Let us refine the very words that articulate our purpose and methods, for within that refinement, we may discover pathways unwalked and unexplored.

With this, we delve into the language that dominates health sciences and the healing paradigm, be it Western or Eastern, alternative or allopathic, allied or conventional, and explore the limitations of what is and the possibilities of what could be. Language is not just a reflection of our healing paradigm, but also the shaper of what it will be to each individual and to society as a whole.

I

On the Importance of Structure

Structure and foundations may seem like an odd place to start a book about language; however, they are the perfect place to start. Historically, the language of every civilisation has been formed and moulded around or by structure, predominately grammatical and societal in nature.

Sting, one of the modern era's greatest and most evocative songwriters, explains that whilst writing songs, he will often finish the music in its entirety before even contemplating the lyrics. He states that 'often when the structure of the song is finished, the story and narrative of the song become obvious'. Within the scaffold of the music, the chords, the harmonies, counter-harmonies, and the timing, there lies a story waiting for words to bring it to life. In this way, structure is not a container for meaning; it is the precondition for its revelation. Many chiropractors have spent thousands of hours and dollars on refining and improving the structure of our communication with clients, noting that it is an integral, if not the most critical, aspect of solidifying a client's compliance with care and achieving best overall outcomes.

If you know me, I'm sure you know that my own verbal communication is something I am determined to improve, and partly how and why these ideas have come to fruition. I've tried numerous scripts and buzzwords, but nothing ever sticks or flows. I feel forced to wing it, explore words, analogies, communication and language that meets the client where they are. This exploration has been a significant part of my consideration of the subjects and topics in this book. I have upset and lost many clients because I spend a lot of time thinking out loud, as if my musician's ear needs to hear my ideas before my brain can properly adjudicate them.

Why is the structure of the language we use to speak to our clients so important?

It's important because, as chiropractors, it's our job: by affecting structure, we affect communication. By affecting communication, we affect function. This is the essence of chiropractic, more so than other healthcare professions. All this still hinges on how effectively and efficiently one can communicate the 'tic' (the philosophy behind chiropractic) with their patients.

The way that anyone approaches a conversation and the language they choose may vary drastically from one individual to another, depending on the nature of their relationship with the interlocutor, where the conversation takes place, and many other contextual factors. However, their speech must still follow a certain set of structural rules to communicate effectively. The importance of structure is witnessed in even the most artistic and rebellious of postmodern architecture, with staircases that lead nowhere and doors that don't open: the foundations must always follow structural regulations, rules of engineering, and the immutable laws of physics. Beneath the surface, the structure is tethered to codes, constraints, and calculations. As the philosopher Ludwig Wittgenstein famously said: 'A serious and good philosophical work could be written consisting entirely of jokes'. In architecture, as in language, as in healing, we may adorn and abstract, but we never escape the need for grounding. Form may flirt with chaos, but function still demands integrity.

'The important thing is not to stop questioning.
Curiosity has its own reason for existing.'

- Albert Einstein -

In terms of structure, from biology to engineering, the following is an observable, immutable, universal truth:

Shape determines function.

This is no metaphor. It is observable at every level of existence: the shape of a thing will determine its function, role, and interactions with the world around it. The form of a protein dictates its chemical affinity, and the geometry of a bone dictates its mechanical leverage. From the microcosmic spirals of DNA to the gross architecture of buildings and machines, the shape of a thing is what enables, constrains, or amplifies its purpose. Recently, I have seen many claim the inverse, that function determines shape, and whilst that is partly true, it is secondary. We are born with an innate shape and design; we can alter that with function. Ultimately though, shape determines function. Hence:

Shape determines function,
but environment alters shape.

This is true of all things. For example, if I take a set of tongs from the kitchen and use them to dig in the garden, they will eventually change shape, most likely folding over and shortening, becoming tougher and stouter, making them better at digging in tougher soils. The environment and function have changed the shape and structure of the tongs. But they are still tongs. Can they do the job of a spade? Certainly, but not as well, and they likely won't last as long.

As we grow, the environments we navigate and the movement patterns we repeat influence the nervous system's developmental and survival priorities. These subtle negotiations between behaviour and biology gradually distort the original design, leading to compensation and, subsequently, to degeneration. Our job is to remember that the original script still exists, however obscured. Healing is not about achieving comfort in a distorted form; it is about realigning oneself to the architecture from which function can once again flow with ease.

> *'The greatest tragedy in science is the slaying of a beautiful theory by an ugly fact.'*
>
> **- Anonymous -**

We have turned a blind eye to many questions as a profession and industry, hiding many struggles and questions beneath the guise of certainty and good intentions. I wholeheartedly support good intentions and the calm assurance of certainty — when they serve as scaffolding for progress, not barricades against it.

Certainty, when wielded with humility, can empower clarity and confidence. But when it hardens into dogma, it calcifies innovation and mutes inquiry. As the philosopher Karl Popper reminds us: 'True ignorance is not the absence of knowledge, but the refusal to acquire it'. Certainty is a guise that all professionals are encouraged to wear, one that our clients expect us to wear. It's comfortable and provides us with a sense of control, self-assuredness and confidence. What better way to sell, than to present with certainty? So, we squash down those little doubts in our minds and push forward.

But what happens if we follow those doubts? Is it possible that those quiet little questions in the corners of our minds are not nuisances to suppress, but invitations to evolve? Could they be the fault lines through which new light enters? Rainer Maria Rilke urges us to 'live the questions now. Perhaps you will then gradually, without noticing it, live along some distant day into the answer'. Society would have us believe that this questioning leads to failure and dissatisfaction in one's career and life, but within those questions — trembling, persistent, inconvenient — might reside the first developing threads of a brighter future, one not yet imagined but already longing to be spoken into form.

The language that currently gives shape to the structure of chiropractic and our healing arts is part of its limitations as both potter and clay. It is as indoctrinated as some of the most tightly held religious notions.

The language of our profession is dictated by the structure of our philosophy, which, for over 100 years, has been dictated by the 33 principles and their inherent worldview. This worldview is one that many, if not most, chiropractors now struggle with or don't even think about. It is one that leads to questions like the following:

If I have healed this issue, why does it still bug me every now and again?

With 30 to 50 years of dysfunction in this body, why have its patterns normalised and peaked in the first four to 12 weeks of treatment?

Can we unlock more, or is this the best we can do?

With human bodies being so similar in musculoskeletal structure, why do primary subluxations vary so much from person to person?

Part of the problem we have in furthering chiropractic stems from the language of our core values, principles and world view. We have unconsciously and unwittingly limited our exploration and growth by founding our profession on an axiom, a defining tenant, that is powerful, effective, and true, but incomplete. By enshrining such an axiom as dogma, we reduce a living philosophy into static doctrine. And as any living system requires change to remain vital, so too must the language of our core tenets evolve if we are to continue growing with relevance, rigour, and resilience.

'The power that made the body heals the body.'

- D.D. Palmer -

This, our founding tenet, is a beautiful statement in its simplicity, depth and meaning. So why challenge it? Why change it? Why probe further? Because revisiting core values in any paradigm and making small, seemingly insignificant changes can often lead to transformative changes. As physicist Niels Bohr once said: 'Every great and deep difficulty bears in itself its own solution. It forces us to change our thinking in order to find it'. A single degree of alteration at the base of a structure may seem negligible, yet it can redirect its trajectory by miles. Likewise, small semantic shifts in our axioms may yield profound clinical and conceptual breakthroughs. We must be willing to entertain the possibility that in our reverence, we may have overlooked subtle but vital dimensions of the healing process — that what is 'mostly true' might still be limiting the truth that is possible.

Why? Because we aren't, by any meaningful measure, winning the war against the degeneration of bodies and genetics. The amount of spinal and skeletal surgeries being had, even and especially by chiropractors, is ridiculous! According to the Australian Institute of Health and Welfare, spinal fusion surgeries alone have increased by over 60% in the past two decades, with a notable rise amongst adults under 50. Despite our claims of preventative care and holistic health, the human frame is deteriorating faster than our tools and philosophies can keep pace. We are witnessing, in real time, the compounding effects of generational dysfunction: babies born with compounded structural deficits, arriving into life already burdened by the unsolved tensions of their predecessors. Whether in the nervous, immune, or digestive systems, what was once considered the starting line of health has now become an inherited battlefield.

So, for the sake of future generations, could we please explore the possibility that there is something else, something more that health sciences and chiropractic could do or achieve? Let us dare to finish the sentence, not to undermine it, but to illuminate its unspoken dimensions. I propose the following refinement:

'The power that made the body heals
and adapts the body.'

At first glance, this seems like an innocuous change, but like a shift in the fulcrum of a lever, its implications are vast. As Archimedes famously proclaimed: 'Give me a place to stand, and a lever long enough, and I will move the world'. A small adjustment at the fulcrum can redirect the energy of an entire system, and so can a subtle shift in our philosophical language reshape the trajectory of healing itself.

The addition of 'and adapts' encompasses so many questions that chiropractic philosophers have been pontificating over for generations: are all subluxations adaptive? If so, could we self-heal all of them with the right stretch or movement? If we can, why does posture deteriorate and the body benefit from adjustments? Does the world even need chiropractors? Does the body only hold adaptations and subluxations that it is currently using? If so, does that make all physical therapists an overpriced band-aid? Will the body remove these subluxations of its own accord when it feels safe/able to?

Or the other line of questioning: are all subluxations traumatic? Can the body not self-heal any subluxation? Is it really that helpless? How do people survive at all without chiropractors? How are they not just a tangled ball of mess and tension by age 30? Or — perhaps more provocatively — is the body not as wise as we credit it? Was evolution right, or did dumb matter just get lucky?

One of the more elegant ways we uncover truth is through the principle of correspondence: what ancient traditions and esoteric sciences refer to as 'as above, so below'. This phrase, echoed through Hermetic philosophy and later adopted by chiropractic, suggests that universal truths echo consistently across all scales of existence. If a pattern is true in the microcosm, it will likely manifest in the macrocosm, and every level in between. It is indeed true that the body heals, courtesy of the power that made it, but it is also true that the body can adapt, courtesy of the power that made it. These same mechanisms and skills are evident all around us every day, especially within our musculoskeletal systems.

Take a complete, displaced fracture of a clavicle, for example. It is within the capacity of the body to heal it, but it would require adaptation that could significantly alter the shape and function of the bone. Hence, if that bone does adapt to that fracture, then there is no hope of the original optimal function of the associated shoulder girdle. As orthopaedic literature affirms, malunion (the healed-but-misaligned state of a fracture) often becomes the new baseline for movement dysfunction (see: Rockwood and Green's (2024) *Fractures in Adults*). It is the same with many aspects of our physiology and biology, including subluxations.

We must therefore scrutinise and assess the impact we are having and have had on the quality of the structure of the human form and its posture, because our posture and structure, much like a language's structure, determine the basis of all future interactions and communications. We cannot continue to settle for the 'average' shape that gives us the same 'within normal limits' rubbish that is thrown at failing bodies by all types of practitioners. If structure shapes communication, then posture shapes perception from both within and beyond the body.

By their very nature, foundations do not beg for attention, but they bear all the pressure. Whether in architecture or anatomy, it is the unseen alignments, the angles, the hidden depths that determine whether a structure holds or collapses under pressure. We intuitively understand this when it comes to buildings, bridges, and instruments. No one questions the need for solid footings beneath a skyscraper, or the precise tension of a guitar neck to produce resonance. Yet when it comes to the human frame, we've somehow become willing to overlook the profound influence that small deviations and unnoticed compensations can have on the coherence of the whole.

In the musculoskeletal system, millimetres matter. Angles carry consequences. A shift at the sacrum reverberates upward, altering rib dynamics, head position, even ocular tension. What begins as subtle drift becomes compensatory overdrive: muscles tighten, not out of failure but out of necessity, and fascia thickens, not from age but from accumulated messages of instability. Precision is not pedantry, it is protection. The same way an engineer will tell you that a beam off by a single degree can change the load-bearing potential of an entire structure, the body too is governed by these principles of alignment and force distribution. We are not immune to physics simply because we are biological.

To ignore this is an oversight. It is to ask the body to carry more than it was designed to bear and then call its fatigue and degeneration a mystery. The curves of the spine, the balance of the pelvis, the orientation of the head and thorax: these are not merely aesthetic ideals, they are functional necessities. They are not dogma, they are design. And to understand healing is to respect the design, to begin again with the basics: the foundation, the angles, the load, the line. Not because we are reductionists, but because integrity begins in the base.

I recently watched a video of a world-renowned chiropractor expressing his frustration with practitioners who reassess long-term, regular chiropractic clients. Specifically, he took issue with those who identify postural distortions in such clients and recommend a renewed corrective protocol, suggesting that doing so reflects poor practice and unnecessary intervention. He implied that if a client is living well and free from pain, then deeper structural correction is irrelevant. He further negated the significance of spinal angles and curves, stating they are often overemphasised. I take issue with these kinds of declarations for three reasons:

1. Perhaps you have missed something. None of us are infallible in our understanding.

2. Significant research and data indicate that end of life and long-term outcomes are directly impacted by postural change.

3. These types of statements are precisely what have stifled the growth and evolution of chiropractic. They reflect a reluctance to question assumptions, to challenge ourselves, and to confront the limitations of our current paradigms.

From a physical perspective, the importance and role of an individual's shape, structure, and posture in communication is well-understood in the art of performance. Many an actor spends hours practicing and perfecting the differing shapes and postures associated with various emotions and states of mind so that they can accurately portray the character. They will spend hours doing this before they even start rehearsing lines because there are unique qualities from person to person as to how each emotion is physically expressed, and this physical communication informs and directs the vocal expression. Each of us moves through the world with a personal lexicon of shape, a signature of posture etched by experience, injury, triumph, and loss. In this choreography of survival, form becomes memory, and structure becomes meaning.

> *'We don't see things as they are; we see*
> *them as we are.'*
>
> **- Anaïs Nin -**

Indeed, a body that cannot flex its thoracic region and allow its shoulders to drop cannot wholly embody depression or anguish. Conversely, a body that struggles to maintain or achieve an upright thoracic posture cannot fully realise the profound expressions of pride or elation. The closer we can restore a body to its original alignment, this primal, sacred geometry, the more effortlessly communication flows within the nervous system. After all, function is a dialogue between organs and tissues, mind and body, self and environment. True healing, then, is not merely about alleviating pain, symptoms, or an individual region's measurements, but about re-establishing this fluent internal conversation by returning the body to the spatial language it was born to speak. As John Philip Newell writes in *Sacred Earth, Sacred Soul*:

> The word revelation stems from the Latin 'revelare', meaning: to reveal, to lift the veil … we are not adding anything new, or something that never existed before, rather we are exposing something that has been lost or forgotten.

This is not a book of answers. It is a lexicon of provocations. A call to precision, to poetry, to participation. Let us lift the veil … together.

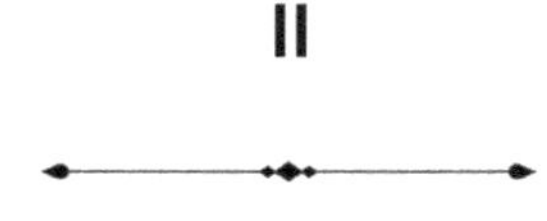

II

Balance + Stability

'[…] a wise man [builds] his house on the rock
[…] a foolish man builds his house on sand.'

- Matthew 7:24-27 -

This statement contains a very poignant truth. It doesn't say you *can't* build your house on the sand, it simply illuminates its foolishness. A person who builds their house upon the sand is constantly patching, straightening, and repairing the shifts and changes that the unstable environment creates.

It has been said that there is no nirvanic state of pure effortlessness or pure stability, at least not until we are dead. The first time I ever heard a statement along these lines was at university, where our biology lecturer would frequently remind us that the only time that we achieve true homeostasis is when we die.

So, let me state this plainly from the outset to be sure we understand each other:

There is no amount of exercise or stretching that can restore a state of true structural stability. It is akin to holding up the house on sand.

When explaining this concept to clients, I use the leaning tower of Pisa as a metaphor. To 'straighten' the tower, one could use ropes and exert considerable effort and increasing tension to balance and straighten the tower, 'training' it. Theoretically, it is doable. But what it is not is an efficient or long-term solution, and it certainly doesn't address the failed foundation: the bedrock upon which real, enduring stability must be built.

This brings us to a central distinction: **balance is not stability.**

'Balance is not something you find.
It's something you create.'

- Jana Kingsford -

Balance is an action, a task. Stability is simply a state of being.

Balance is a dynamic and performative act, a constant interplay of feedback loops and micro-adjustments. You can balance on a tightrope, but you can't build a home there. Stability, by contrast, is a platform. It is rest and presence. It is trust in the structure to hold, without constant vigilance.

Our modern obsession with balance masks our lack of true stability. In our quest for balance, we've grown increasingly reliant on an ever-expanding arsenal of rituals and tools: daily exercises, stretching routines, saunas, ice baths, meditations, medications, orthotics, ergonomic shoes, posture-correcting beds, beds that shift and elevate, chairs that cradle or even lift us to our feet, and a dizzying catalogue of supplements designed to stave off discomfort and dysfunction. All of this to maintain the illusion of equilibrium in an environment that is anything but stable. And yet, when our systems inevitably reach their threshold and begin to unravel, we either act surprised or blame it on old age — as though our compensations weren't just deferring the collapse.

'The body remembers what the mind forgets.
And it remembers through tension.'

- Bessel van der Kolk -

Take, for example, a recent client of mine: a seasoned, world-champion, Olympic rower. As impressive as his accolades are, he now finds himself unable to jog, run, or even stand comfortably for extended periods of time, even though he still rows tens of kilometres each week. Years of elite training carved a neurological and structural hierarchy in his body: one where the act of rowing became paramount. Through repetition and the reward of achievement, his nervous system and structure prioritised this singular function, sacrificing the biomechanical adaptability required for broader patterns of movement. In optimising for mastery, his body has inadvertently narrowed its functional repertoire.

This is the body's hierarchy in action. The body, like society, runs on inherited logic. And this survival drive often means that compensation is not dysfunction — it is brilliance at a cost. The brainstem mediates survival postures. The sympathetic nervous system handles arousal. Even when 'still', a body balancing under duress is not actually resting. This is observable in EMG studies showing hyperactivity in stabiliser muscles (e.g. multifidus, transverse abdominis) in individuals with postural asymmetries or chronic instability (Hodges & Richardson, 1996). They're always 'on'.

'Nature does nothing in vain.'

- Aristotle -

Your body is not dumb. Its hyper- and hypo-tonic muscles and subluxations are not mistakes. Stability means that the system no longer needs to perform, hold, or remember elaborate tensions for base function. It means the spine does not need to hold compression or over-extension to maintain vision or balance. This in turn means that you cannot train muscles for true structural stability.

Like a house built on sand, muscle and fascia are the visible, surface negotiators of change. They are the windows that no longer open smoothly, the doors that don't quite meet their frames, the cracks through paint and plaster. All of these are signals, not of faulty windows or stubborn doors, but of a foundation quietly shifting beneath the line of sight. Bone, like the true footing of a house, rarely announces itself. We do not tend to see it, we seldom acknowledge it, and it has no direct way to speak. There are no sensory nerves within the bone itself. By the time the walls complain, the ground has already moved.

Let's talk about Byron Bay — the place that has been my home for more than ten years and is, to my mind, one of the most unique and curious places on earth. It has an even more curious history, and that history is central to where my train of thought originates.

When my wife, Megan, and I first moved to Byron, we anticipated — much like most fresh-grad allied and alternative therapists — that working here would be easy. Surely, an 'enlightened and healthy' population would welcome us with open arms. Surely, we'd be stepping into a like-minded community ready for what we had to offer.

Ahh, the naivety of youth.

As chiropractors, Megan and I found ourselves in a strange cut in the community: too mainstream for the hippies, too hippie for the mainstream. Either way, we were often the last-ditch effort from both sides, neither wanting to admit that their lifestyles had 'failed' them. What began as a frustration became a kind of apprenticeship. That awkward in-between place forced us to excel at our craft and gave us a rare education in how different groups — spiritual, scientific, religious, sceptical — think about health and healing.

Byron has always been considered 'ahead of the curve' in many ways, health and healing among them. Whilst most large populations drift toward inactivity and lethargy, Byron tends to push people to the other end of the spectrum: overactive and overstimulated. Many of my clients can perform extraordinary tasks under pressure, but when they stop, they collapse. They break. The holiday reveals the fragility. Stillness becomes the stressor. Time away from exercise or productivity exposes the unaddressed storm within.

Our unstable bodies become like bicycles: they feel safer in motion than at rest. Some people are so wired they can only cope if they keep moving, others are so depleted that any additional demand is simply too much. In them, stress breaks a system too weak to cope. In both cases, the same truth emerges — balance is not peace.

It is effort and strain. It is a muscular, cognitive, and emotional expenditure. We remain 'balanced' only as long as we have the energy to hold ourselves there. When that energy runs out, we fall.

The Indigenous history of Byron Bay, and its role for the traditional custodians of the Northern Rivers region, adds another layer. A conversation with a local Aboriginal elder once filled in a crucial piece of lore for us: the Byron Bay township area was, and is, a sacred meeting place where many local tribes would send members of their communities who needed healing. It was referred to as 'a place of healing and madness', because it was understood that if a person did not give themselves over to the healing process here, they would go mad. That lore is still observable in the way people move through this town today.

*'The visible world is the invisible
world made manifest.'*

- Sri Ramana -

Byron is a place built on the notion of 'going with the flow.' In traditional Chinese medicine, the water element dominates winter, and winter is considered the season of healing. Byron Bay is dominated by water. It is a subtropical region with high rainfall, wrapped in some of the most beautiful beaches on the planet. It is a place where you could swear the saturation of the world has turned up to eleven.

Places like this exist across the globe, places where the 'veil' between the physical and the energetic seems thinner. Other places of amplification include the Pyramids of Giza, Stonehenge, and the Grand Canyon. Colours feel brighter, contrasts sharper.

Recessions hit harder, but good times fly higher. It often feels as if God has installed a tap here with only two settings: completely on or completely off.

Pre-Covid, Byron Bay, with a local population of roughly 8,500, would consistently open its doors to over 2.5 million tourists each year. The town itself is incredibly transient. Locals would jokingly place bets on newcomers, the so-called 'blow-ins,' guessing how long they'd last, anywhere from three to 36 months. It seemed cynical at first, but over time it became observably true. People move to Byron for a transient, existential chapter of their lives: to heal, to find themselves, to reinvent. They either do the work and move on, or they get chewed up and spat out. Between the 2016 and 2021 government censuses, more than half of Byron's population had changed. I suspect the next census will show an even greater shift. Byron has an uncanny way of testing the mettle of those who arrive with dreams of becoming someone new.

> *'The fluid requires the container.*
> *Without structure, there is no flow —*
> *only spillage.'*
>
> **- Thomas Hübl -**

Without a stable structure, flow slowly degrades into chaos. Under the seductive banner of 'go with the flow', often reinforced by boundary-less childhoods and well-intentioned but misinterpreted Eastern mysticism, uncomfortable and difficult experiences are taken as signs that you are not 'in flow' and therefore should be avoided.

We have had many patients flow into our clinic, wide open to possibility, and then promptly flow back out once they are confronted with structure and its importance, whether that is the structure of scheduled appointments or the importance of their physical structure. The very things that might hold them are the things they resist.

The Taoist texts speak of *wu wei,* effortless action, but even that rests upon a deep internal order. This, I believe, is a common trap for those pursuing flow or balance as the ultimate goal. Balance is wondrous and useful. It can yield incredible growth, adaptability, and achievement. But it is not where we heal. Our deepest and most meaningful healing comes from firm foundations, stillness, and calm. Whilst many a leak can be plugged whilst you are out on the water, true healing and correction require pulling the boat into dry dock and attending to it properly. Once that work is done, entering and sustaining a 'flow state' demands far less effort.

My years in Byron have repeatedly reinforced this: the people who achieve the outcomes they came here seeking (healing, self-improvement, genuine transformation) are not the ones who chase ever more flow, but the ones who are willing and able to connect beneath the water's surface and anchor themselves to something solid.

Of course, the things we need most are often the things we most resist. Confronting something uncomfortable triggers memories and reactions of times when you were flooded with uncomfortable thoughts, poor self-control, weakness, or pain. That's what makes it uncomfortable. It is understandable that you would avoid that. This movement around and away from the unknown or the uncomfortable is deeply human, and in a place like Byron it is easily reinforced.

But whilst we are busy pursuing and maintaining flow, we are actively and constantly engaging the systems and mechanisms that keep us 'balanced'. Helene Langevin's research into the biomechanics of fascia suggests that myofascial tissues require rest and decompression to sustain their health and responsiveness. Without pause, the body's capacity to heal is not just diminished, it is biologically thwarted. When we are on 'dry land', when structural demands and sensory inputs are dialled down, the workload on those balancing systems is significantly lessened. Only then do we create the environment in which healing is truly possible.

Let us stop glorifying tension. Let us stop treating balance as the endgame. Let us reimagine healing not as an ever-expanding to-do list of self-regulation, but as a returning home to the place where little effort is required.

Having treated and observed many chiropractors and long-term chiropractic patients, I rarely see much difference between them and someone who has maintained a good diet and some regular biohacking habits. Yet if we were achieving all that we claimed we were, this should not be the case. If the skeletal system fully regenerates every seven to 10 years, why do people who are being regularly adjusted, still end up with similar end-of-life mechanics and degeneration as those who aren't? This issue has become progressively worse over recent generations despite many of these practitioners having fabulous diets and lifestyles, and it's not like gravity is getting stronger.

Humans have a very well-documented history of trying to restore and maintain balance in environments that were fundamentally unstable. In the financial sectors, in governments, the pharmaceutical industry, and in nature. We have a habit of looking at symptoms and, with an intense commitment, waste immense amounts of energy and time trying to counteract them. Introducing new animal or plant species, trying to reduce carbon, bailing out banks, printing money, giving more power to governments and regulatory bodies, more laws, more 'education', more safety protocols, more 'research', more exercises… And what have our efforts achieved? More stress, more division, more tension, less foresight, less health, and less stability. Every structure that we created to serve and protect our sovereignty, our individual and societal stability, has been mutated, manipulated into institutions that now cause more issues than they alleviate. It really is no wonder that children are growing up with so much depression and disease. What hope would they have when they see the way we have become enslaved to these dysfunctional institutions? Some might argue that this is through design, that there are powers or people who want to destabilise society for their own gain. 'Control through chaos', or some such nonsense.

Some people saw this coming a long time ago. These words came to us from Malcolm Muggeridge in the 1970s:

> So the final conclusion would surely be that whereas other civilizations have been brought down by attacks of barbarians from without, ours had the unique distinction of training its own destroyers at its own educational institutions, and then providing them with facilities for propagating their destructive ideology far and wide, all at the public expense. Thus did Western Man decide to abolish himself, creating his own boredom out of his own affluence, his own vulnerability out of his own strength, his own impotence out of his own erotomania, himself blowing the trumpet that brought the walls of his own city tumbling down, and having convinced himself that he was too numerous,

laboured with pill and scalpel and syringe to make himself fewer. Until at last, having educated himself into imbecility, and polluted and drugged himself into stupefaction, he keeled over — a weary, battered old brontosaurus — and became extinct.

We know inherently that our society teeters on the edge of complete collapse and chaos, but for the time being we seem to be maintaining some semblance of 'balance'. I would say that society in Western civilisation as a whole is in a pre-acute phase. This, I believe, is why so many people are taking to 're-wilding': alternative currencies and off-grid living. People, consciously or subconsciously, can see the writing on the wall and are looking to stabilise their individual worlds' foundations outside of our corrupted existing structures.

Systems and environments can be both balanced and unstable. When you're stable, you are also balanced. When you're balanced, you're not necessarily stable. Medical and health sciences did some early research about homeostasis, the naturally occurring process of the body's desire and search for balance, practitioners had some early wins, and so we all stuck to it like white on rice. This is a rabbit hole that the health sciences world has fallen into, and we really don't know what to do now that we're seemingly at the bottom and realising that it's not getting the job done.

Why are we stuck in this rut? I believe it is because we have never had clear differentiations between 'balance and stability', 'healing and adaptation', and 'stress and trauma' within the physical therapies. In lieu of this, we have had to become clever at tracking and affecting as much as possible. Without clear definitions, and thus differentiation, how do we know what we are affecting?

How do we assess a nervous system? We want to know how stable it is, how robust it is, and how much free space there is to deal with day-to-day life. A stable system can push and exert itself just as comfortably and easily as it can sit in stillness and do nothing. It can sit and journal just as easily as it can go to the gym. It can tighten and strain as effectively as it can relax. Our conscious and subconscious minds simply know what they know, and they want what they know. Rarely do they know what they need. Our subconscious craves familiarity, the well-worn path. So, we often find ourselves back at the gym, or in front of the television in a subconscious pattern of avoidance until life forces our hand.

The brainstem, being home to our deep reptilian survival instincts and mechanisms, has very different priorities to our conscious and subconscious brains, as per *Our 3 Brains* from Dr. Paul Maclean and Dr. Scott Walker. It is what drives and controls our musculoskeletal tensions and changes for the sake of survival and safety. Taking optic and proprioceptive information, accounting for every bit of your individual history being stored and carried in your body, it will modulate function in order to best survive the environments that it's exposed to. According to Dr. Stephen Porges's polyvagal theory, cues of safety, especially those perceived through embodied states like posture and breath, engage the ventral vagal complex, enabling social connection and physiological restoration. A major driver for our return to familiar settings or states.

And this brings us to chiropractic. It is not just the cracking of bones or the restoring of motion or even the stimulation of nerve signals. It can be a re-introduction of integrity and stability, an embodied message that signals safety to the nervous system. In trauma-informed care, this principle is echoed: the body must first feel safe before it can fully heal. Structure, then, is not just biomechanical, but also relational, neurophysiological, and symbolic. A spinal realignment, an adjustment, a correction, is a shift in the system signifying that you are safe now, and you can begin to release. You can stop compensating. You can let go. When we restore the spinal alignment to its original centre, bit by bit, the mind, spirit, and life can do the same. There is less balance, and greater stability.

III

Stress + Trauma

'Between stimulus and response, there is a space.
In that space is our power to choose our response.
In our response lies our growth and our freedom.'

- Viktor E. Frankl -

'Trauma is not what happens to you. Trauma is
what happens inside you as a result of
what happens to you.'

- Dr. Gabor Maté -

Stress and trauma are not the same thing, and there is a very real, understandable and simple difference between them emotionally and physically. Let's start by looking at what our current definitions are for these words:

'Stress: a state of mental or emotional strain or tension resulting from adverse or demanding circumstances' (Center for Health Advocacy & Wellness, 2025). This is not good enough. Can stress only be mental or emotional?

Dr. Hans Selye offered up the most well-rounded definition I could find: 'Stress is the nonspecific response of the body to any demand for change'. This is good, very good. It speaks to the nervous systems generalised 'fight, flight, freeze, fawn' response that is activated in preparation for changes in environment.

Let's see what the ever-faithful Oxford Dictionary consensus is on trauma:

'Physical injury.'

Great. What does that mean, specifically? Physical injury requiring hospital or otherwise significant intervention? Stitches? Bruising? A strain? A scratch? A subluxation?

Here again, Dr. Selye has provided us a decent, yet incomplete definition, he refers to trauma as 'distress': '**Distress** is the condition that results when stressors produce maladaptive responses when the adaptive energy of the organism is depleted or disordered'.

Stress and trauma are the inescapable companions of a life lived, carved into the sinews of our stories, our nervous systems, our relationships. Here again, our practice has suffered due to a lack of linguistic clarity. A necessary delineation needs to be made and accepted between them before health sciences can see big breakthroughs in their treatment and understanding of the body.

> *'There will come a time when our descendants*
> *will be amazed that we did not know things that*
> *are so plain to them.'*
>
> **- Seneca -**

This linguistic issue has existed in the physiological sciences since Dr. Selye first introduced the word 'stress' in the mid 1900s to health sciences. It baffles me that up until this point, there was no defined term for *stress* in relation to an individual! In fact, it wasn't really until the late 1950s that the word really became familiar in Western lexicons. At this stage, the term was favoured by mental and psychosomatic sciences and therapies, but not physiological. It was considered too abstract and unmeasurable. Since then, it has remained elusive and opaque. We all agree that there are some stressors that are traumatic and some that aren't; Dr. Selye categorised these two forms of stress as distress (negative stress) and eustress (beneficial stress). However, we have no explanation for why these two forms exist, nor do we have clear boundaries between them.

Dr. Selye's work and definitions around eustress and distress are very well-rounded. Unfortunately, it's not language that is used in our popular lexicon and there's a piece of the puzzle missing that has prevented physical therapists from implementing and utilising this wisdom practically. We will use subluxations to illustrate this from a chiropractic perspective:

> Subluxation: A vertebral subluxation occurs when the joints of the spine fail to move properly causing interference with the nerve messages from the brain to the body and/or from the body to the brain. This can affect movement patterns, muscle balance and even the function of organs and the chemicals and hormones they produce [...].
>
> **NZCA**

Is a subluxation a trauma, or just an adaptive stress? Maybe it causes and maintains stress and dysfunction in the system. Could subluxations be both trauma and stress? Do we have the same level of nuance in the art of physical healing, or are we just adjusting everything outside of 'normal limits'? Different chiropractic techniques have varying justifications and theories as to why the subluxations they correct are the 'right ones', or, as we frequently refer to them, 'primaries'. Some of these justifications are incredibly convoluted and watery. Every therapeutic intervention has its reasoning and philosophy, some weaker than others. None are complete.

As proud men and women of science often do, we have a habit of throwing in many complicated words and theories to make an argument sound more robust than it really is. We often stick to these ideas and concepts much longer than we should.

I'll be the first to say that I can often get stuck inside conceptual black holes for longer than necessary. I'm sure any sane person who knows me would probably say I'm stuck in one at the moment. I hold much respect for the people that pursue these rabbit holes, whether I agree with them or not. There are very few people in the world who can withstand the social pressures telling us to avoid said holes; fewer people still are ever able to emerge after having been to the bottom. Often the work and investment that we put into getting to the bottom of a thing makes removing ourselves from it seem insurmountable or too humbling, and so we justify staying there. The isolation that we require to get to the bottom becomes its own form of comfort due to its familiarity. Chiropractors and chiropractic have done this many times in many ways. These thought processes are a necessary part of our evolution, we *must* dive deep down theoretical and hypothetical rabbit holes to find the truth of the matter, even if it's just a sesame seed's worth.

However, a trap that swallowed up the physical therapy industry early on is the habit of referring to stress as either 'good' or 'bad', which is an inherently flawed concept to begin with; it's like calling emotions good or bad. They aren't good or bad, they just *are*. We know that the subtleties of the human body and nervous system are much more intricate and complex than just 'good' or 'bad', 'too much' or 'too little', and so on. Most of nature's behaviours fall into this realm of complexity, existing outside of our concepts of morality. For example, going to the gym isn't simply a good stress or simply a bad stress; it's just a stress, and it is often both good and bad simultaneously. It can facilitate both growth and decay at the same time. But again, why? And what's the difference?

Our definitions of 'stress' and 'trauma' are so vague and archaic that it really is no wonder why our physical therapies have struggled to get out and away from this concept and evolve over the last 100 years. Health sciences and physical therapies, chiropractic included, haven't really made any massive leaps or bounds since the Thompson Drop technique in the 1950s. Consequently, the human population is plummeting into decay physically and genetically. The percentage of our population still requiring skeletal surgeries is embarrassing, and the growing rate of neurological degenerative diseases is staggering. We have found some innovative ways to use technology for biohacking, assessing, and otherwise facilitating our jobs. But we are still doing, at a base level, the same manner of corrections and interventions we were 80 years ago. Stuck in a rut. Stuck in a rut. Stuck in a rut. It really is no wonder that as a culture, our focus has shifted toward emotional and mental healing whilst tolerating the body's ageing and degeneration.

To address the lack of clarity between the concepts of 'stress' and 'trauma', I propose the following definitions:

> **Stress:** Something that causes your body to alter its function and position away from optimal but **within**

the limits of innate self-correction. Stress is a change that one **can** self-heal.

Trauma: Changes that alter our body's function and state **outside** of those limits of self-correction. Trauma is a change that one **cannot** self-heal.

What happens when we encounter a trauma? We adapt! We utilise and employ stress that we can control to compensate for the trauma we can't. Both stress and trauma can be created within the body, by the body as part of its survival instincts. We see this same process mentally and emotionally, particularly in addiction. The addiction is not the original trauma — it's the adaptation in response to trauma. It's an example of stress that is controlled to cope with the trauma that cannot be controlled.

Why are these definitions vital? They indicate that even small changes away from the 'ideal' can be indicative of significant underlying dysfunction — dysfunction that we are only now starting to better understand. In all aspects of health (psychological, biological, and sociological), we are starting to better understand that surface level changes are often just signals. Chiropractic as a profession has been saying this since its inception; it is based on this very idea. It is not a foreign concept to us, but we never took it far enough within our own framework. We have just assumed that subluxations are the 'end of the line' and as such, that if a subluxation exists, it must be the root cause and must be corrected. We see changes in the system that correlates to a specific vertebra and assume that this vertebra needs correction. That it and its changes are not in and of themselves a correction.

Some practitioners talk about primaries and secondaries, but these are always unique to an individual. And yet, nearly all humans have the same 'ideal' postural position. The same ideal mechanical and structural position. The same bones, the same muscles in the same places doing the same things. This inherent ideal mechanical, structural, and postural position comes gifted with an innate range of motion (ROM), strength, and function. The more we focus on the ROM, strength, and function, instead of the core mechanical, structural, and postural position, the further away from the 'ideal' we fall. Stress is expressed as outcomes, but the trauma is in the foundations.

In bloodwork, it is now possible to link specific changes and patterns to genetic, parasitic, viral, bacterial, or dietary issues with much more accuracy and nuance than we ever have. This allows us to sort through the weeds and differentiate between stress and trauma in our bloodwork, allowing treatment to return the client to a more effortless and natural state, as opposed to treating each blood marker individually once 'normal limits' are exceeded (as most medical practitioners have for the last 70 years).

Stress can be great to utilise and expose oneself to. It is how we expand ourselves and test our limitations. I imagine it sometimes to look a little like a fence line or boundary, except that it's a self-healing elastic. In order to expand our boundary, and thus capacity, we must apply stress to the fence. Once we have taken it out a step, we let it settle and stabilise before taking it further. The problem occurs when we try to push too far, too quickly. Our subconscious has to recruit from, and subsequently compromise, other areas in order to facilitate this desired growth or goal. Stress becomes trauma, and something that may be hugely beneficial and even 'healing' in one aspect of our self could be traumatic to another.

Take surfing, for instance. There are many benefits to surfing, but it also takes a very heavy toll on the body. The sustained hyperextension whilst on the board paddling, akin to doing a workout whilst lying on your stomach, is then paired with heavy rotation and torsion motions whilst riding the wave. It is an inherently damaging activity for our skeletal system, but like most of life's activities, there is also good mixed in with the bad. Our muscles are strengthened by the stress, and it yields many benefits for our mental and biochemical health. As such, many don't realise the damage that is being done until it's too late and they are having to give up the short board for the long, or the long for the stand-up paddle, or the stand-up paddle board for retirement.

Few will argue that for the majority of the population, our greatest capacity for health is in our early years. For most healthy children, movement comes effortlessly from the good posture that also comes effortlessly. I frequently hear adults talking about how resilient the young ones are, lamenting the loss of their own capacity to 'bounce back'. What don't we have in these younger years? All the learnt survival mechanisms of an older nervous system, all the learnt mental and physical adaptations. The collections of dysfunctions that manage and stem from our unhealed trauma from all sorts of obvious and discrete sources.

All manners of trauma are unavoidable in life: emotional, spiritual, and physical. Indeed, it's the topic of much thought and art. Many creative and philosophical pursuits convey the value of pain, discomfort and even sorrow:

> *Sorrow is better than laughter: for by the sadness*
> *of the countenance the heart is made better.*
>
> **Ecc 7:3 KJV**

Author David Whyte, in his book Constellations, writes of pain that it has an unmatched ability to return us to the present, to a state of humility and into the open arms of previously resisted support.

Avoiding trauma is not the goal of a life well lived. Rather, how we deal and what we do with said trauma seems to be a stronger defining feature.

One of the aspects of trauma that has provided a limitation on our understanding is a societal expectation that trauma is a big, obvious event where a dramatic change happens suddenly. This assumption subconsciously dictates that healing should happen similarly. A one-off event with fireworks and a dance troupe! This idea likely originates with the concepts of 'miracles' from on-high, where the local priest would come to your house with holy water and pray with gusto on your behalf for healing, and that was all that could be done in many cases. Prior to antibiotics and anaesthesia, our knowledge and practices didn't hold favourable outcomes for acute scenarios. This show and theatre was hijacked by medicine and science. You go to the hospital, a chapel to disease with stark white lifeless interiors, big bright lights, gowns, faceless shapes dance around you as you drift into the void and are brought back having been 'healed'. We now expect healing to be an epiphany or a sudden moment in time, equal to that of our expectations of trauma. Sometimes it is, no doubt, but give me the long and winding road that gives me the best view along the way. This would probably be a good place to put a story about a rabbit and a hare.

Another way of observing the difference between stress and trauma is through the present. Stress in the musculoskeletal system is a short-lived tension pattern relevant to the environment and its stimuli. Unhealed trauma presents as chronic changes that persist beyond environment and stimuli with symptoms presenting

somewhere other than from the point(s) of traumatic change. It frequently happens in practice, for almost all practitioners, that a patient with issues in an area left untreated can experience functional or symptomatic improvement.

Practitioners of traditional Chinese medicine sometimes care little for the vast majority of 'symptoms' because they recognise them as messaging signals from the body indicating that something is not right. Sometimes, these signals and messages tell us very little about what's actually wrong. Your tight shoulders could be due to dysfunction in almost any joint or combination of joints in the body; the tension creating the pain could be triggered by a mental or emotional response. The tight shoulders are just a symptom, a messaging signal. Are there issues in the shoulder? Undoubtedly. Could we adjust the shoulder to 'switch off' the signal? Certainly, but the body isn't so daft that it would send its messages with the lame bird. No, it will give the message to a bird with the capacity to deliver the message safely, or as safely as possible. To force the body to turn that signal off may prevent you from finding out what switched it on in the first place.

One man's trash is another man's treasure. Just as
one man's stress is another man's trauma.

Trauma sits on a scale much like stress: there are big obvious traumas, like car accidents, and there are smaller, less significant or obvious traumas like sitting in a poorly positioned car seat for too long. What is traumatic to one person may not necessarily be to another, this will depend on the individual's capacity and resources. In terms of emotions, I think much of it comes down to parenting. Have you been shown or taught how to healthily process and deal with this emotion in this environment?

An interesting concept and idea to consider is that we have the ability to cope with trauma by creating trauma. It is often the avenue our subconscious leads us down after it has exhausted other alternatives, or if the trauma is significantly overwhelming. Usually, later into our years, as the space and robustness in our nervous system has been tensioned and twisted, many activities we do can trigger traumatic compensations in our system. This is an unfortunate place to be and requires much diligent work to remove ourselves from this precipice. Again, I would encourage you to consider this beyond the physical — this is a response or reaction we can often see in our relationships and emotions. For example: when we don't know how to feel and process grief, it can turn into anger or something else that we do know how to process.

Stress and trauma are unavoidable. They are, in fact, a necessary part of life. A keen understanding of what they are and their differences will, over time, with honest and genuine curiosity, lead us to new techniques, treatments, and interventions that can more accurately and efficiently diagnose and treat the condition that we have long considered 'old age'.

IV

Healing + Adaptation

We are much like a tree against the wind: it changes us, as we change it. The wind strengthens us as it weakens us. In the same way, our adaptations strengthen us and weaken us at the same time — more so if left unchecked. Much like wind to a tree, life is infinite. There is never going to be a time when wind ceases forever. We adapt and mould to suit the prevailing winds over time, strengthening ourselves against them, and as we age, we weaken to the inevitable cross winds as they expose our weaknesses. Therein lies the danger of unresolved adaptation.

All living things rely upon two survival mechanisms: healing and adaptation. It is curious that in the world of health sciences, rarely do we consider these mechanisms within the systems of the individual at the physiological and musculoskeletal level. In fact, we often consider them interchangeable, as if they aren't two separate mechanisms at all. This omission is not just theoretical — it has clinical consequences. Without recognising how these mechanisms operate and interact internally, we remain limited in our ability to differentiate between what the body is attempting to resolve and what it is making itself endure.

It seems almost as if we have come to view only external environmental changes or factors to be traumatic, and that there are no internal changes that the body cannot self-correct or self-heal. We speak of the body as though it were an unfailing mechanism, equipped with infinite self-corrective capacity, as if there are no internal thresholds that once crossed, lie beyond the reach of our inherent capability. But every system has its edge, and not all wounds are worn on the skin. Some reconfigure our foundations silently, shaping posture to impact our perception and physiology without ever reaching conscious awareness. Instead, they show up in fatigue, neurological deficiencies, fascial distortions, and digestive dysfunctions: quiet markers of a deeper rupture.

'The shortcomings of a profession are at once the most empirically verifiable reality but at the same time the most intellectually resisted fact.'

- Adapted from Malcolm Muggeridge -

The words 'healing' and 'adaptation' have been used for many scenarios, sometimes accurately, often not. Where did our definitions stem from in this modern age?

Our cultural roots in religion, be it ancient spiritual traditions or the more recent sacraments of science, have left deep imprints on our understanding. Once upon a time, both healing and adaptation were seen through spiritual lenses as grace and endurance respectively. Healing was long seen as proof of divine favour, an ethereal act belonging to the gods. Adaptation, by contrast, was viewed as man's gritty compromise, a necessary struggle in a fallen world. Chiropractic has held and carried the message of innate intelligence for the last 120 years. However, has chiropractic's veneration of innate intelligence helped or hindered our understanding of healing? On one hand, it has continued and carried the powerful understanding that the body is intelligent, dynamic, and designed to heal. On the other, it may have led us to overestimate what the body can overcome without assistance and underestimate the cost of adaptation when healing does not occur.

During chiropractic's early development and adolescence, the medical union/lobby group that is the AMA (American Medical Association) was already a dominant political force due to its financial backing and impact on battlefields with its use of penicillin and anaesthesia. Alternative and traditional therapists very quickly found themselves on the back foot, David against a Goliath that could move as quickly as Usain Bolt. The challenge and nature of our foe is part of the reason we have missed the mark on healing, the pressure we felt to 'keep up' with medicine. As such, we developed techniques that would allow us to compete. Medicine set the terms of engagement, and we played along. It is often said that what we resist, persists. In our effort to resist medicine and provide a point of difference, we unwittingly gave it power over us. Maybe it wasn't avoidable. Maybe it was the tax of surviving next to a louder god. Industrialisation, telecommunication, mechanisation all hail speed and productivity. Healing, once a mysterious and sacred act, was recast in the mould of mechanised output. We just followed suit. We treated clients with shoulder pain at the shoulder and those with low back pain in the low back, working to improve the symptoms, ROM, and function of those areas, but rarely considering the cost it was having on the rest of the body. Modern chiropractic graduates are now inheriting a confused puddle of half-baked philosophy and field-tested techniques that work more often than not.

> *We often just assume that because we have achieved symptomatic resolution naturally, that we have facilitated healing.*

This is a logical fallacy. For example: chronic stress leading to cortisol adaptation. The person no longer 'feels stressed' because their hypothalamic-pituitary-adrenal (HPA) axis has down-regulated responsiveness. Yet physiologically, their body is carrying the silent toll of allostatic load (McEwen & Wingfield, 2003). We know that symptomatic resolution isn't a complete definition of healing, and yet it remains the biggest and most frequently utilised unit of measurement for a majority of health and healing modalities, including chiropractic. So, what is the difference between healing and adaptation?

Healing: The mechanism by which a system or individual releases or corrects stress or 'change of function' that is no longer advantageous or necessary for survival.

Adaptation: The process by which a system or individual employs stress or dysfunction in order to survive a stressor that cannot be self-healed.

It is clear that at every level, in every one of our systems, we can heal some things and not others. Hence, sometimes we heal, sometimes we adapt, or we die. Yes, external environmental factors have a role to play, but if we are fully self-healing entities, why don't the subluxations or changes created in response to a stressor not release or resolve as soon as we are out of that environment? The answer may be that we cannot make the necessary changes to our own musculoskeletal system to facilitate healing.

You can't see your own blind spots.

That's why chiropractors, health practitioners, and healers have jobs in the first place: if we were fully self-healing entities, no healing practitioner would ever have existed. Our bodies would only ever temporarily change shape or function for an environment, and then, once removed from the environment, be back to their perfect selves.

When society's genetics and lifestyle were much less burdensome, our physical interventions and techniques were enough for the population of the time. That's not the case anymore: the genetics, nervous systems, and lifestyles that we are passing onto the next generation are woeful, and they certainly aren't getting stronger by any broad stroke. Adaptation is a mechanism that science has been discussing for quite some time and is most commonly referred to as a mechanism of evolution: a species' long-term altering of genetic attributes for survival in changed environments. Yet it also exists in short term scenarios as we all see frequently. It is a wondrous ability that has served nature in a magnificent capacity for thousands of millennia.

However, both short- and long-term adaptations have a cost. When trauma impacts our ideal structural positioning, the brain and body get to work — they adapt. They reroute and plasticise. They reallocate tensions, alter proprioception and vision, chemistry and build new patterns of movement. They bend us to preserve what matters most: survival. It's somewhat ironic, isn't it? The same patterns and changes that enable us to stand and survive in the face of trauma and challenge are the same patterns that create our degeneration and chronic dysfunction. The same functions and activities that we use to increase our capacity, to stay feeling good and 'young', often drive our degeneration.

When we look at the abilities that the body has had to adapt, we see a striking resemblance to the ways in which a musician or audio technician can alter frequency.

'If you want to find the secrets of the universe,
think in terms of energy, frequency, vibration.'

- Nikola Tesla -

Interestingly, all of the following affect the shape and structure of the wave form:

Expansion: The process by which we grow and expand our capacity to cope and deal with life.

How do athletes continue to perform with often significant underlying dysfunction? By expanding their capacity with training at an obsessive rate. Expansion is a young person's game.

Modulation: The process by which we can alter our perception or experience of something in order to better cope and survive.

We insert orthotics into a client's shoe to alter the walking experience, so that the load and dysfunction is spread up the mechanical chain and away from the tender, failing plantar fascia.

Regulation/limit: The process by which we can contain or limit our experience within our 'safe' or 'normal' limits.

The self-imposed boundary, such as 'I guess I'm just getting old, I probably shouldn't try that again'.

Compression (Consolidation): Condensing changes as a matter of efficiency, observed as reduced spinal disc height and is often emotionally expressed as 'pushing it down' or 'swallowing it'.

This adaptation, used to create stability, is observed even in young and healthy spines, suggesting it's not solely due to a lack of adaptive ability or old age.

These four methods of adaptation are great tools that are useful to have access to, both individually and as practitioners. And of course there are more. The nervous system is an artist of survival. Give it a problem and it will find a brush. We see these intelligent mechanisms every day: antalgic positions that allow us to stay upright and mobile, flu symptoms that facilitate detoxification, inflammatory responses that supply necessary healing components to damaged areas, vomiting and diarrhoea that remove toxins from the digestive tract. These things are stress and dysfunction that our body utilises for survival. Maybe we need to reassess our use of the words 'dysfunction' and 'maladaptation'.

We have worked diligently, mastering the art of adaptation, but have barely scratched the surface of healing. When we deliver adjustments with the primary aim of restoring movement, triggering nerve response, expanding range of motion, or alleviating pain in a specific joint complex, we may achieve relief but not necessarily healing. These outcomes, though laudable, can often represent adaptations: the body's incredible capacity for plasticity, not its return to coherence. In many cases, we are not addressing the origin of the dysfunction, but merely its latest echo.

Many practitioners profess the greatness of innate intelligence and then proceed to 'correct' as many changes as possible in an individual's body. Why? Because it often feels amazing, Dr. George Goodheart is noted for saying that if you see a stress, fix a stress, and if you see dysfunction, correct dysfunction. Whilst I deeply respect Dr. Goodheart's genius and contributions to humanity, statements like this one inadvertently undermine the very intelligence we claim to honour. It implies a lack of intelligence within the body and its changes; it undermines the core message that chiropractic and kinesiology have sought to elevate. His statement implies that our innate does not or cannot use changes of function (states of 'dysfunction') intelligently or intentionally, and cannot correct these changes of its own accord. However, we know that this is not correct.

Adaptation left untreated, becomes dysfunction.

Dysfunction left untreated becomes identity.

Adaptation is most profound and obvious in bodies that have done any activity, particularly strenuous activities, frequently over a long period of time. Ballerinas are a wonderful example. We've all had that unmistakable moment when a new client steps into the clinic and before a word is spoken, their history speaks through their form. 'This woman was a ballerina,' we think, not read from any chart or intake form, but derived from the unmistakable shape etched into her posture, the way with which she moves, the mechanics of her gait. Unfortunately, she is significantly more likely to develop scoliosis than her non-dancer counterpart. One study found scoliosis prevalence among elite female dancers to be nearly twice that of the general population, suggesting a link between prolonged asymmetric loading creating ligamentous laxity and the development of structural spinal changes (Roche et al., 2012). Surfers are another great example. For the die-hard, daily surfers, it's not uncommon to watch their backs become as stiff and straight as their surfboards. Interestingly enough, put either of these two types of people into regular physical therapy and/or chiropractic care for an extended period of time, and you know what their posture looks like by the end? The same, or worse.

Our unconscious, survival (reptilian) brain has a very different set of priorities from our conscious or even subconscious brains (as posited by Dr. Paul MacLean's triune brain model). Its main priorities are focused on survival, including what is necessary to stay upright and keep moving forward. It will sacrifice many functions and tolerate and utilise many dysfunctions in order to maintain base survival capacity. For chiropractors, this means that the body will create and maintain subluxations as part of its survival processes. This change in spinal joint positioning for the sake of survival is achieved by muscle tension changes, reinforced and held long-term by fascial changes. This is why many physiotherapists and fascia-based practitioners, like osteopaths, can claim their point of contact as the progenitor of trauma. So close, and yet, so far. Muscles and fascia are the container in which trauma is held, but not its originator. Many of these practitioners, because of their professions' own socio-political histories and limitations, also lack the training to assess and correct the skeletal issues.

The same 'adaptation = compromise' principle plays out beyond just the musculoskeletal mechanics of an individual. I would suggest that we also have a similar principle at play spiritually. Whilst it's not something we can validate, it's acknowledged and recognised in dialogue throughout the world and its histories. It's the hidden, latent cost that hits us where it hurts — a 'deal with the devil'. We make these trades because survival (perceived or actual) demands it, until at last, the cost exceeds the gain. Someone, or something, comes knocking to collect. In many circumstances and environments, adaptation is the fastest and easiest road to comfort, but as David Whyte writes: 'Comfort is a beautiful servant and a dangerous master'. Each of us needs to ask, are we restoring youthfulness with every visit? Or just making the decline more comfortable?

Subluxations *are* an expression of innate intelligence. The hubris of our profession has inclined us to believe that we know better than innate intelligence. We have, with much gusto and enthusiasm, done the child's homework for them. The child got great grades and performed excellently, right up until they were left to their own devices.

A relative of mine found themselves stuck in an unfortunate loop of care because of our outdated philosophies and practices. After a bad accident resulting in severe daily neck pain, she sought chiropractic care and found that manual chiropractic adjustments to her upper cervicals would provide great relief. So, she followed her outlined care plan, a perfectly justifiable plan, to the letter. Unfortunately, over time she became reliant on these regular adjustments for relief, what started as a schedule of recovery and correction became a daily band-aid.

We have all manner of biohacking devices, tools, remedies, supplements, and techniques, each proclaiming to be the final key to healthy lifespan and longevity. None of them can address or create the necessary 'unlearning' environment for the neuro-musculoskeletal system like chiropractic could. We keep trying to bully and coerce our nervous systems into submission with stronger or altered interventions, failing each time to unlearn the accumulated patterns. But this much is clear: unless we honour and understand the body's innate intelligence to a significantly greater level, no intervention, however sophisticated or spiritual, will take us beyond the threshold to true restoration.

Charles Darwin noted that 'it is not the strongest of the species that survives, nor the most intelligent, but the one most adaptable to change'. The shortcoming of adaptation is its cost. It's a carried cost, often hidden, and the longer we have and hold the adaptation, the higher the cost becomes for us and our offspring. Adaptation is akin to 'robbing Peter to pay Paul', as my wise mother would say — stealing from your long-term to feed your short-term. This is because in this field, 'adaptation' is synonymous with 'compromise'. We sacrifice a little from places that our subconscious survival centre deems less important to improve function in another area under greater demand. The more demand we put on that area, the stronger it gets and the more compromised other areas become as we sacrifice to meet increased demand. Biomechanical efficiency is traded for biomechanical necessity. Over time, flexibility calcifies into fragility.

Dr. Patrick Gentempo's concept of General Adaptation Potential (GAP) extends Dr. Hans Selye's pioneering work on stress into the somatic realm. According to Dr. Gentempo, each person has a finite reserve of adaptive bandwidth. As subluxations and compensations accumulate, this reserve dwindles and the spinal cord torsion rises. Complexity compounds. The pursuit of allostasis exhausts us. In contemporary physiology, the concept of homeostasis is an ageing one; an updated suggestion is that of allostasis. Coined by Sterling and Eyer (1988), allostasis refers to the achievement of 'stability through change' (p.636). Unlike homeostasis, which seeks a narrow range of constancy, allostasis acknowledges that the body is designed to adapt, although not indefinitely.

Allostasis is the price of survival.
But allostatic load — the cumulative
cost of adaptation — is the price
of chronic imbalance.

- Paraphrased from the work of McEwen and Wingfield -

This is observed in our young. The nervous system of a child is, in the majority of cases, the best it will ever be throughout its lifetime. Children don't need to stretch for ideal range of motion; they don't (and shouldn't) need to go through months of patterning and rehabilitation for a good squat position or movement mechanics. They possess full, effortless function across the board (albeit with a lack of muscle mass). This explains the resilience of children: their adaptive reserves are wide open. They can bend, twist, fall, and recover. But today, with epigenetic and environmental burdens, many young people are born already significantly compromised, with methylation (detox) and mitochondrial (energy) dysfunctions as well as neurological and developmental issues. By our mid-twenties, much of our adaptive currency has been spent.

A pivotal question that the health sciences have failed to answer, and seemingly even consider, is: if the human body's primary form (musculoskeletal configuration) and base function (survival) are mostly identical between individuals, how then can one individual's primary musculoskeletal issues, or even primary subluxations, vary from someone else's? The answer is that every human form has the same inherent limitations in its design that are simply accentuated by an individual's capacity or environment. What makes us unique is not our inherent limitations, but the patterns and the way we react and respond to those boundaries being crossed. The Stress-Diathesis Model suggests that our inherent biological vulnerabilities interact dynamically with environmental stressors, and that individuals differ primarily by their adaptive or maladaptive responses (Monroe & Simons, 1991). It's an idea that many spiritual and religious ideologies and philosophies share, that we are all from the same spirit, the same spark of awareness, the same source, just living a different experience. A concept echoed in physics through quantum entanglement, unified field theory, systems theory and ecology. There are undoubtedly, in all aspects of our being, many factors for consideration as to what determines an individual's 'faults' and an issue's root cause, but we all have them! Our innate design comes with inherent flaws and weaknesses, but individually we have differing capacities. We also share the same emotional flaws and weaknesses with differing capacities: anger, jealousy, greed, pride etc.

Dr. Jesse Jutkowitz's work with Advanced Bio-Structural Correction has evolved our understanding of humanity's inherent structural limitations in a direct and meaningful way. Its simplicity is beautifully refreshing. According to Jutkowitz, 'primary biomechanical pathologies (subluxations) are those that the body cannot self-correct' (Advanced Biostructural Correction Teaching Materials, 2024). As such, any subluxation or musculoskeletal change that the body *could* self-correct is secondary to the aforementioned primaries. It is there because the innate intelligence is utilising its change of function or position.

Muscles too tight? Secondary.

Fascial distortion? Secondary.

Dr. Lowell Ward (Spinal Stressology Technique), and later Dr. Jesse Jutkowitz in his development of Advanced Bio-structural

Correction, demonstrates a confronting yet compelling anatomical reality: between C7 and L5, the only *primary* spinal subluxation is an anterior vertebral shift. Put plainly, if a vertebra moves forward, it is beyond the body's innate corrective capacity. There is no muscle, nor combination of muscles, that can pull it back. The design simply doesn't allow it. Some spinal faults can be self-corrected because muscles can pull them *against gravity and against the line of load.* But an anterior shift is different. The body can brace around it, stiffen above and below it, torsion the ribcage, rotate the pelvis; yet none of those strategies are a true posterior translation. Whether you agree with the absolute claim or not, the principle stands: there are structural changes the body can stabilise brilliantly but still be unable to reverse.

What does this mean practically? If you lie face down on a table and a practitioner presses your spine into the surface, the structure will momentarily comply. You may feel neural stimulation, a rush of proprioceptive feedback, even hormonal excitement, the body's familiar cocktail of adaptation. And yet beneath that transient buzz, the architecture is weakened. Force may create sensation, but sensation is not correction.

This is an uncomfortably disruptive idea for many practitioners. And yet, with even a moment's honest reflection, it is a logical conclusion. If this idea feels unsettling, sit with it. Explore it. Let it disturb the mental furniture a little.

> *'Healing doesn't happen when we're managing symptoms. Healing happens when the system no longer needs to produce them.'*
>
> **- Deb Dana -**

Healing is such an unconscious and natural part of our system's function that it happens before we are even aware of it. By the time our conscious mind is aware of tension, weakness, and tingling, our body has already healed what it could and is now using symptoms to signal to us that a boundary has been crossed. Given time, energy, and space, your subconscious will find adaptation pathways to create comfort in its dysfunction, but this ultimately weakens the body.

One only needs to look at massage therapy to observe this paradox. Massage, when administered intentionally, skilfully and at the right time, can offer profound relief and energetic or emotional healing. It can soothe nervous system arousal, restore circulation, and promote release and trust. Touch itself is an ancient and essential modality for healing. But massage, like any intervention, is not neutral. It can just as easily disorganise as it can balance.

At the neurological level, muscles are never self-willed. They respond to stimuli: emotional/chemical, environmental, or structural. All muscular tone and activity are downstream of the nervous system's perception. When we repeatedly use massage to suppress these muscular signals without addressing their origin, we risk falling into the same trap as when we rely on overly soft beds, orthotic shoes, or supportive chairs. These tools offer comfort within dysfunction. They accommodate maladaptive patterns and, in doing so, deepen them. A massage that releases muscle without stabilising the underlying structure can create a brief sensation of freedom, only for the nervous system to panic and reinstate protective tension more aggressively. Why? Because the muscular bracing that was released served a compensatory role. A state of ease that is unaccompanied by foundational structural support or environmental integrity is not just temporary — it can be dangerous. Make no mistake, *most* subluxations that chiropractors 'correct' fall into this category and frequently have similar responses.

We say that health is about vitality and the ability to thrive, which is a wonderful sentiment, but how do you measure that? Is it fitness? Strength? Hormone health? Gut health? Intelligence? Creativity? Are you looking at how white and clear my eyes are? How true are the colour of my eyes? The texture and tone of my skin?

Rather, I would define 'health' as the most effortless expression of one's fullest capacity. This perspective highlights the fluid nature of our existences, emphasising how humans are can adapt to and be influenced by the environment or circumstances in which we find ourselves. Optimal health is expressed by one's ability to express and move with seasons and environments. So, if health isn't simply 'a lack of symptoms', why do we still consider healing to be the removal of symptoms? This then brings us to ask: what is *true* healing? It's the process of unlearning; it's the effortless release of compensations and adaptations. It is the restoration of general adaptation potential which can be measured by the relaxed postural alignment of our structural foundations, our bones. There should be with every session a noticeable improvement of the body's upright postural mechanics.

We have all witnessed the progressive growth in psychological and emotional healing over the last two decades. Physical healing could be informed and guided by that framework, as it really is way ahead of our institutionalised treatment protocols when it comes to musculoskeletal healing. Our roles as practitioners who wish to facilitate this healing process is to create a stable environment in which the system feels safe and able to release and forget these compensations physically.

This is not always an easy process, though. Have you ever tried to pull a child's special toy or blanket away from them when they were feeling agitated, sensitive, or scared? Not an easy task. Releasing physical survival mechanisms can be just as difficult, emotional, and reactive for some people. I wish it were an exact science, and maybe one day it will be, but between a client's uniqueness, practitioner errors, and the occasional false positive, the process can be extremely challenging at times for both practitioner and client. Some of the adaptations have been in place for years, having been instilled under very precarious and highly emotional times of life, creating a strong sense of reliance on them and a fear of what will happen when they aren't there. Of course, the vast majority of clients aren't consciously aware that this is why they are scared or hesitant about the process or a correction. This is an idea Dr. B. J. Palmer, one of the founders of chiropractic, explores in tone and timing. If the current configuration is being actively utilised by your nervous system in its survival, will it let go? Will it correct? Oftentimes, the answer is 'no'.

'You can't heal what you won't feel.'

- Resmaa Menakem -

If you have been following even loosely the world of neuroscience and psychology, the 'response versus reaction' concept has been quite the field of intrigue over the last few years. Reactions are considered a knee-jerk, learnt survival mechanism driven by our sympathetic nervous system against any manner of stimulus or stressor, but when an individual is operating from a place of parasympathetic 'calmness', they have much more control, a choice, over how they *respond*.

Unlearning reactions is therefore involved in healing the nervous system. In fact, it is *the* pathway for healing the nervous system. Carried through by an 'as above, so below' method, structural healing is facilitated through the same unlearning process. If we look at Pavlov's dogs, we see this displayed for us in the phenomenon of response extinction, which *is* nervous system healing. Meanwhile, adaptation keeps the memories, tensions, and subluxations that already exist and adds something on top, not requiring the client to let go of the current configuration completely, but enabling it to find balance with it. As stated earlier in this book, there is no amount, or type of exercise that can create true structural stability or healing.

Chiropractic, I believe, is optimally suited to spearhead the evolution and exploration of these developing principles.

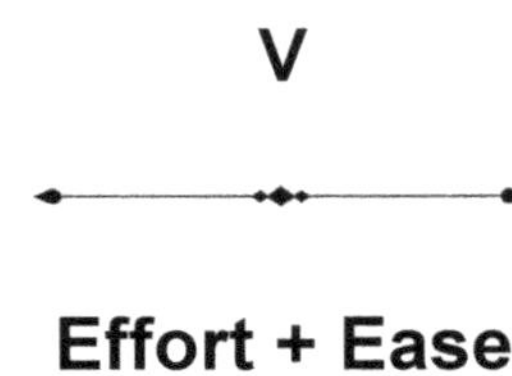

V

Effort + Ease

'From the mouth the heart speaks.'

- Luke 6:45 NKJV. -

Across the broad spectrum of human ideology and social discourse, from the far reaches of the political left to the unwavering tradition of the right, there exists an embedded truth, a seed of validity. As humans, we often hold tightly to ideas that are not full truths. Ideologies and discourses are not illusions or fabrications: they are partial perspectives rooted in real needs and historic conditions. Whether born of aspiration or discontent, most movements and opinions arise from attempts to make sense of a world that rarely offers clarity. Yet, when these part truths are mistaken for whole truths, when they become dogma rather than inquiry, distortion follows.

Eventually, what catches up with us all is the reality that nothing comes without cost. Every choice, every action, every omission, every pursuit of what is good, and every rejection of what is harmful exacts something in return. Actions have consequences. This phrase is often used in situations where the proverbial other shoe has dropped — something unwanted or undesired has occurred.

There is no limitation in the statement to that, though. Indeed, 'actions have consequences' reminds us that there is no purely 'good' or purely 'bad' action. Every action has both 'good' and 'bad' consequences. The universe does not discriminate between noble intention and careless impulse when it comes to causality. Healing is no different. There are obvious costs in money, energy, and time, and there are less obvious costs, such as dysfunctions that have become identity, and social pressure to conform.

The human impulse to seek resolution often overreaches; in our desperation to preserve what matters to us, we often discard everything around it. Thus, we fall into the archetypal trap of 'throwing the baby out with the bathwater'. This reactive purge is what fuels the great cultural and societal pendulum. Some chase the water, others the baby, and some are left clutching nothing but an empty bucket, bewildered at how they lost both. This is not an issue limited to the uneducated, in fact, it is often less dominant in this demographic. We, the educated health practitioners, are often even more stubborn and iron-willed than the next person.

Speaking of iron-willed, the importance of a good work ethic is a very proud point for my father, and whilst I am known to occasionally whinge about the younger generation's lack of work ethic (with a definite sense of self-deprecating irony), it does point to the idea that life shouldn't have to be constant struggle, effort, and output. Yes, there's struggle, and there should be. We need it, and it's good for us. However, the younger generation is not interested in the end-of-life health complications that come with the idealised hustle approach of its predecessors. Nor are they interested in the often-found dissatisfaction and failings in their personal lives that coincide with a life dedicated to constant output. Further, the younger generation's general health would likely not permit such levels of output, partly *because* of the hustle of their predecessors. Practicing in Byron, I have seen and worked with numerous health and life coaches who have made hustle and grind the definition of their image, and I can tell you now that it doesn't end well. What begins as performance enhancement often ends in adrenal fatigue, autoimmune conditions, or emotional dissociation.

The same 'hustle' mentality has been a cornerstone of the health and medical industries for well over 100 years. From a young age, individuals seeking to work in these fields are aware that they have a long and arduous road ahead of them. It's no surprise, then, that our treatment methods and protocols frame and position us as gods or as taskmasters to those for whom we provide our services and knowledge. Our expertise bolsters our hubris to the level of divine miracle worker, or our desire to shirk all responsibility for any unwanted outcome demands that our clients complete an extensive list of daily exercises, stretches, and tasks.

Western medicine, shaped originally by religious notions of humanity's inherent weakness was refined and sharpened by Darwinian mechanistic assumptions, which view the body as a broken machine in need of intervention. Evolution is portrayed as chance-based and indifferent. In these views, the body is flawed and ultimately dependent on external correction. Science is framed as modern salvation, the tool by which we override our biological inadequacies. On the other end of the pendulum, Eastern and New Age paradigms take a different approach, often veering into the equally problematic territory of idealised self-sufficiency. These perspectives suggest that all healing resides within the self, that one must simply manifest, breathe, and allow. Whilst empowering in theory, this viewpoint can unintentionally diminish the importance of support, community, structure, and skilled intervention whilst isolating an individual. As patients, Western medicine strips us of power, but also responsibility. Eastern medicine gives us back the power, overwhelmingly so, and is often laden with guilt and shame. They are the poles of ease (Western) and effort (Eastern). They are not in conflict; they are complements. Healing, in its truest form, exists at the intersection of effort and ease, of intentional action and receptive capacity.

Healing lies not in willpower, but in willingness.

As our world becomes more unstable and the pendulum swings a little further each way, individuals are required to either exert increasing effort to form and defend their opinions, or succumb to societal pressure and swing with the pendulum from one pole to the other. Neither end of the spectrum possesses the whole truth, no matter how much it is declared to be 'their' truth. As my mother would frequently remind me: there are two sides to every story, and then there's the truth. I've grown to appreciate the gravity of that statement more with each passing year. It's a nod to nuance, to mystery, to the reality that complexity resists simplification.

It should be made clear that effort and ease are not entirely synonymous with tension and relaxation. There are many similarities and crossovers, but they differ in intentionality and capacity. In fact, they have a lot to do with balance and stability, with the performance and the effort involved.

Seeking ease is not inherently an assurance of a healthy or resilient body. This phenomenon extends far beyond bodywork, reflecting a pervasive cultural narrative. We see it echoed in familiar idioms, such as 'lulled into a false sense of security', which describes our collective vulnerability to illusions of ease and resolution. The appearance of comfort, when not supported by authentic coherence or structural integrity, becomes a seductive mirage.

It offers temporary reassurance yet ultimately blinds us to the underlying instability. This illusion misguides the client and can lull the practitioner into complacency, mistaking transient softness for sustainable change. Without anchoring interventions in contextual coherence, both practitioner and receiver risk mistaking sensation for transformation. Think: soft beds, shoes, chairs, and constant massages.

Our physical, postural patterns and habits are deeply reflective of our mental, emotional, and biochemical behaviours. And, as with our psychological tendencies, the path of least resistance prevails. It is easier to surrender to a sugar craving than to pause and metabolise the discomfort of restraint. It is easier to lash out than to regulate our internal state and choose a tempered response. It is easier to gamble on the thrill of a quick return than to invest patiently for long-term growth. This is why past injuries linger in memory and in movement. The body, when left without the opportunity, resources, or environment to properly heal, defaults to what it knows. It is protective. It returns to the familiar pattern, the compensatory shape, the protective adaptation. Creating a new, coherent strategy demands energy, safety, and coordination. Familiarity breeds comfort, and reusing the old path, even if it is dysfunctional, is neurologically more efficient. Practice doesn't make perfect; practice makes permanent. This is why, when we want to facilitate healing beyond the last known point of comfort, we must be willing to prioritise what a system needs over what it wants.

For instance, we have all had patients come in and try to direct the course of an appointment by telling you that they know exactly what they need to feel better. Things that have worked in the past for similar symptoms. Sometimes this is the case, but often it isn't, and rarely will it lead to healing instead of further adaptation. One must be willing to confront stored and ignored dysfunctions in order to progress beyond the immediate state of dysfunction and environment.

One of the pivotal moments that led me to question the actual healing capacity of a classic subluxation adjustment unfolded during a walk on the Byron Bay lighthouse circuit. Descending a steep incline, I stepped onto the rough edge of the path and rolled my ankle severely, the movement accompanied by a loud, unmistakable 'crack'. The sound was sharp enough to elicit a gasp from the people behind me. In the moments that followed, I experienced a profound flood of hormones, creating a temporary euphoria despite what had just occurred, and a rush of clarity. It wasn't until several hundred metres later, as I continued walking relatively pain-free, that the pain signals caught up and inflammation began to set in. I eventually limped into the ocean to soothe the emerging rigidity and swelling. This experience left a deep impression. It wasn't just about the injury, it was about the sequence. The delay. The hormonal cascade. The initial ease followed by lockdown. It prompted me to explore a hypothesis grounded in evolutionary logic, and to reflect on what it might reveal about subluxation, adjustment, and the sensational patterns we observe in chiropractic care.

In the precise moment that I roll my ankle, my brain has not yet constructed a complete picture of the injury. In response to this ambiguity, and in anticipation of potential threat, it initiates an immediate hormonal cascade. This neurochemical response, primarily mediated by the HPA axis, results in a surge of catecholamines and glucocorticoids that temporarily enhance mobility, blunt nociceptive input, and facilitate escape or continued movement (Sapolsky, 2004). This hormonal cascade is an adaptive evolutionary buffer, serving as an emergency override that allows the organism to flee danger before it fully processes the trauma. At the same time, the sudden mechanical stretch of peripheral tissues and abrupt proprioceptive input through muscle spindles and mechanoreceptors initiates a reflexive signal to the central nervous system, what we might interpret as a neural 'reset' moment, triggering rapid reassessment and reorganisation at both spinal and supraspinal levels (Proske & Gandevia, 2012).

If we apply this model to the chiropractic adjustment, the parallels become compelling. Spinal adjustments can provoke cortical changes, including increased sensorimotor integration, improved prefrontal cortex activity, and altered somatosensory processing (Haavik & Murphy, 2012; Lelic et al., 2016). These findings suggest that a clean, well-delivered adjustment may elicit a similarly potent neurochemical and neurophysiological response: a temporary state of heightened awareness, cortical re-engagement, and altered proprioceptive prioritisation. The joint may align more closely with textbook ideals, and the client may experience significant symptomatic relief.

A core tenant of manual therapies that remains under-investigated is whether such interventions truly resolve the traumatic change that initially gave rise to the subluxation. We may interrupt the pattern, but do we dismantle its originator? In not doing so, we find ourselves repeatedly climbing halfway up the hill of healing, only to slide back down into dysfunction. At best, we slide more comfortably. I believe this is why some people love the cavitation, or 'crack', from a chiropractic adjustment and some people loathe it. It is neither good nor bad, but some nervous systems don't want to find out which it could be. Many, if not most, chiropractors still only consider a correction successful if they have created a cavitation.

Food provides a striking parallel to skeletal adjustments and the healing spectrum of effort and ease, serving as both a literal and metaphorical illustration. Just as some interventions can be profoundly restorative whilst others are deceptively harmful, food can span the gamut from deeply nourishing to insidiously toxic. We consume foods that are truly healing: rich in bioavailable nutrients and minimally inflammatory. We also consume foods that are technically 'healthy' but can easily lead to overindulgence, disrupting metabolic balance through excessive intake or poor digestive compatibility. Some foods may appear satisfying but offer little to no net benefit, taking more from the body in processing than they provide in sustenance.

A good example is that of anti-nutrient-rich foods. Compounds such as phytic acid and lectins, found in legumes, kale, and certain grains, can inhibit the absorption of essential minerals like calcium, iron, and zinc (Hurrell & Egli, 2010). Whilst these foods may register as 'filling' or even beneficial in a broad dietary context, their biochemical effects can paradoxically deplete the system over time. The metabolic cost of digesting these substances can exceed their nutritional return, especially in individuals with compromised gut function. This mirrors therapeutic interventions that feel good or produce short-term symptomatic relief but ultimately draw on the system's adaptive reserves. The danger lies in mistaking satiety or stimulation for nourishment.

And so, following the path of least resistance does not equal healing. This is supported by a growing body of research demonstrating that as people age, those who do not engage in regular resistance or weight-bearing exercise experience significantly higher rates of physical frailty, which includes muscle atrophy and loss of bone density. This increases susceptibility to falls, fractures, and reduced functional independence (Mitchell et al., 2012; Westcott, 2012).

Longevity and vitality require more than comfort. They depend on structured, intentional engagement with appropriate stressors that stimulate the system to strengthen and increase capacity.

Healing is a survival mechanism gifted to us by God. It is, in fact, our favoured form of survival, preferred over adaptation. As such, it rarely requires 'conscious' effort and energy. It comes from a deep, unconscious part of our being, often without us realising it. It is an autonomic function, along with digestion, breathing, and sleeping. We do not consciously direct white blood cells to a cut, nor do we coordinate the release of clotting factors or the migration of fibroblasts. The body responds instinctively, assembling a cascade of biochemical repair with astonishing precision.

Healing is invited through stability, not achieved through struggle. Our capacity and ability to heal are largely, if not completely, dictated by the stability of our environments. This is not because effort is inherently harmful, because, as discussed, effortful practices such as strength training enable longevity. However, chronic or acute effort activates pre-conditioned responses in our motor patterns and emotional reflexes. The subconscious mind does not distinguish between what we call 'good' stress and 'bad' stress. It simply recognises the *possibility* of a threat and responds with patterns that have ensured survival in the past. Modern neuroscience supports this: the brain's limbic system, particularly the amygdala, functions as a pattern recognition tool, detecting cues based on past associations rather than objective rationality (LeDoux, 2003). Once a perceived threat is activated, the autonomic nervous system enlists familiar survival strategies, bypassing more integrative cortical input. This is one reason why we default to familiar reactions under pressure — they are neurologically preloaded as efficient coping mechanisms. Hence, the healing environment must support *deactivation*, not merely of stress itself, but of the patterns that stress reinforces. If you want to help a ballerina heal their structure, they need to stop dancing for a time, just as surfers need time away from surfing, and slouchers need time away from the couch.

The more we learn about the brain, the more we see how closely the nervous system resembles the technology we build. Think of the brain like a computer: your nervous system is the operating system and the hardware it runs on. You arrive with a set of defaults: some strong, some flawed, and a body with limited capacity. As life happens, especially through stress and trauma, you build "workarounds" (adaptive code) to keep functioning. These don't erase what came before; they sit on top of it, taking up more space and energy, increasing base level output and requirements. Healing occurs when we can delete the old code, so the system can run cleanly again. This 'deletion' is otherwise known as 'response extinction' in Pavlov's work.

A concrete example of over-effort is the use of unstable seated positions, such as exercise balls or balance-challenging chairs. Whilst often marketed as tools to improve posture and core strength, they do so by imposing continuous proprioceptive demand. This sustained sensory input overrides the brain's natural postural autopilot, constantly forcing conscious engagement of core musculature and stabilisers. Over time, this results in heightened neural tone and behavioural rigidity. Individuals that have spent long periods of time in such seated arrangements often look, and subsequently behave, like they have a stick up their butt. As discussed, our neuromusculoskeletal systems hold patterns of personality. Rigidity in the spine manifests as rigidity in persona. Slumping in the shoulders becomes emotional withdrawal. Form frequently precedes both function and identity.

One of the important mechanisms in mental and emotional healing is the *lack* of connection between our memories and our body clock. It is why things that happened 30 years ago can seem just as real to our system now as they did at their inception. The healing process for emotions and emotional reactions does not require the individual to psychologically walk back, step by step, through the changes that have occurred since the pattern was established. We are able to reproduce the physiology and the reaction at any time, providing us with the environment and stimulus to correct said reaction. Our musculoskeletal mechanisms are heavily connected to our internal clocks, and so every shift that our bodies make is in sequence. Taking into account our full physical histories of what's stored, our bodies add adaptative changes sequentially. As such, the healing process requires us to walk *the body* back through these changes in the sequence in which they arose, or at least close to. Depending on how your body has collated and compartmentalised its patterns and responses via the 'stimulus generalisation' mechanism (Pavlov, 1927), sometimes seemingly 'random' symptoms can arise.

> *'The brain is a prediction machine. When it cannot predict safety, it defaults to protection.'*
>
> **Stephen Porges**

When it comes to healing, less is more.

This 'effort and ease' relationship is reflective of the numerous different environments at play in any given moment. Through Dr. Scott's work with the Neuro-emotional Technique (NET), we know that to clear neurological pathways we need multiple facets in play:

1. The emotion (stressor),

2. The environment (stimulus),

3. Correction (input for reset).

These neurological requisites also form the basis of structural or postural correction. With this framework in mind, I believe this is why prone, facedown 'adjustments' cannot facilitate structural healing. Yes, the joint can move in this direction to an extent; however, there is no neuromuscular precedent for this. Our pathways and environments are not geared around, or for, lying prone. Not only that, but it is likely impossible to create the right angle and generate the right force to correct an anteriorly shifted vertebra whilst a patient is lying prone. Our human design and subconscious programming is set to keep us upright: seated or standing. This is the environment we are designed to live and excel in; this is the environment we want to correct in.

At least once every two months I have a tourist come through who tells me that I'm unlikely to get a cavitation from a certain area, usually T4–T8. They went to the biggest, strongest practitioners they could find, and no one could get it.

Then I adjust them standing, and it goes off like a firecracker.

Not because that's what I necessarily wanted, or needed, but because I was working with the body's natural positioning and tensions rather than against them. It is also frequently surprising how little force or thrust is needed to facilitate a structural correction when the environment and angles are correct.

Healing, then, is not the triumph of discipline over the body, nor is it the surrender of the body to comfort. It is the art of selecting the right degree of demand, at the right time, in the right environment, and having the humility to let the organism do what it already knows how to do. Sometimes the most skilful intervention is not another layer of effort, but the removal of noise: fewer inputs, fewer variables, fewer performances disguised as progress. This is where ease becomes earned, not purchased. Not the narcotic ease of avoidance, but the clean ease of coherence.

For the practitioner, this demands a different kind of leadership. Not the taskmaster, and not the passive witness, but the steady hand that can hold a client at the threshold where effort and ease meet. To know when to ask for more, when to ask for less, and when to ask for nothing at all. Because in a world obsessed with feeling better quickly, the real revolution is learning to become stable enough to heal slowly, stable enough to let the old code delete, stable enough to tolerate the quiet, and stable enough to choose what the system needs over what it wants.

Final Thoughts

So then, what is our path forward?

We are not healed by insight alone. Nor are we healed by repetition. We are healed when the system can sustain both without contradiction. It's true of the body, and true of our professions. Can we hold the past without it choking our future?

Each of us must begin our path forward by determining if it is indeed a path and journey we wish to embark on. As I have stated many times, the pursuit and facilitation of healing is not the path for all therapists or clients. Many will, and should, continue as they are, serving their community in the same ways they have always done. For those individuals, if I could gently bring an honest awareness to the truth of their interventions, I believe that it would provide a wonderful basis for progress. Our next step is to be able to honestly assess our work and determine whether we have indeed facilitated a healing and stable environment within our clients' structures. To this end, I have created an online course that goes through the process of teaching one how to assess the overall structural function and integrity of a body, which can be found on my website www.reganosborne.com.

No longer will the labels and identities of 'mechanistic', 'vitalistic', or 'holistic' carry any significant value; already people are losing interest in these terms and the ambiguity surrounding them. Instead, we might align ourselves to 'adaptive' or 'healing' subtitles and identities, defining ourselves by the pre-existing processes with which we prefer to work and assist. Each approach has pros and cons for each individual, and they will differ from client to client at different stages and seasons of their lives.

The pursuit of balance mirrors the elusive quest for happiness. Neither inherently flawed nor futile, this pursuit nevertheless reveals its limitations when envisioned as a permanent destination rather than a fluid, transient state. Literature abounds with contemplations of happiness as ephemeral when chased, slipping further from reach the more vigorously it is pursued. True, sustainable happiness, the kind that nourishes the soul and grounds our lives, rarely arises from deliberate striving alone. Instead, it blossoms organically from a life deeply rooted in purpose, richly infused with love, and gently steadied by structure. It emerges most beautifully when we cease the restless pursuit, allowing ourselves to simply live with intention, presence, and grace.

So, after all is said and done, the mechanists were correct. The vitalists do have a tendency to 'over-adjust' the body, and indeed possibly to its detriment. But the vitalists were also correct — the human body is one single environment, and you cannot affect one aspect without it affecting another. Every practitioner in the world, Eastern or Western, is a holistic practitioner whether they want to be or not. The greater risk lies obviously with those that do not acknowledge it as such, but we all can facilitate improvement in one area by compromising others, and we all have. We didn't watch closely enough. I see it now though, I observe someone being adjusted by another practitioner and watch the reduction and restriction around the lungs increase with every posterior to anterior prone adjustment even when the patient sighs with relief.

The two techniques that have prompted and driven this book are the Neuro-Emotional Technique as created by Drs. Deb and Scott Walker, and Advanced Bio-Structural Correction as created by Dr. Jesse Jutkowitz. Both of these are built upon other amazing techniques that are worthy of exploration: Kinesiology by Dr. George Goodheart, the Total Body Modification (TBM) technique by Dr. Victor Frank, and Spinal Stressology by Dr. Lowell Ward. As such, I would not dare to imply that these two techniques alone are capable of creating a healing environment in either mind or body. With that said, in my experience, there is a unique efficacy with which they can achieve it.

Healing through stability is not just a concept. It is an observable reality echoed through generations of religious and philosophical texts and concepts, discussed in the halls and forums of environmental and psychological sciences. It is both a neurostructural signature and a physical state. It is the rhythm of restoration and the true north of every healing journey. It is what we reach for in every exhale that finally lands, in every stillness that does not collapse, in every movement that feels like remembering. Polyvagal Theory suggests that ventral vagal activation (the physiological basis of safety) can be observed in the tone of voice, the softening of facial muscles, and the spontaneous depth of breath (Porges, 2011). This is why setting an atmosphere and expectation for safety and stability in your clinical spaces is vital to achieving the best results. It is also why the state of mind and stress levels of your patients can have such a dramatic effect on physical outcomes from session to session.

Stability is not perfection. It is not necessarily symmetry. It is not even regulation in the way we've come to expect it. It is often just a quiet shift in the alignment between mind, body, and environment. And in that moment, however brief, the system finds rest. Not because everything is resolved, but because nothing is in conflict.

The deliberate and meticulous employment of language as an instrument for transformation is far from a novel philosophical revelation. Throughout history and particularly in phases of conquest and expansion, civilisations have harnessed language to shape societies, redefine communities, and reconstruct perceived realities. Frequently, it is the subtlest recalibration within the very foundations of language that yields the most profound shifts, cascading through human consciousness to radically alter our collective trajectories and outcomes.

Language plays an essential role in our returning to coherence. It is both tool and terrain. Words shape experience as they describe it. They become the scaffolding through which perception finds form. As Wittgenstein reminds us: 'The limits of my language mean the limits of my world'. We must pay careful attention to our language and what it is saying about our profession and our daily practices.

> *'Words are, in my not-so-humble opinion, our most inexhaustible source of magic.'*
>
> **J.K. Rowling**

It is not the rupture that defines us. It is our capacity to repair ourselves and the manner in which we do so. To retrieve ourselves from the scatter. Healing, in this light, is not an event, it is a journey. It is not a solitary activity. It is a threshold, a dance. A return to that which was veiled by trauma and our responses to that trauma. To the unbroken stream of self that existed before the compensation, before the override, before the dissociation. Before the body became a site of performance rather than presence. Peter

Levine suggests that 'trauma is not what happens to us, but what we hold inside in the absence of an empathetic witness' (Levine, 1997).

Coherence does not ask that we fix everything immediately. It asks that we stop fragmenting ourselves further. That we stop applying patchwork to a pattern that needs to be unwound. That we stop reinforcing the scaffolding of survival when the architecture of ease is waiting to be restored. We must train ourselves, as practitioners, to recognise this state of coherence. To trust it. To protect it. To know its signs and its silence. To know when the body is releasing, not simply regulating. Our current modus operandi: 'to facilitate balance and comfort' will not provide our communities the assistance they need for much longer. Our world is pleading for someone, or a collective of someones, to give shape and guidance to this deep yearning that is observable at every level of our societies and cosmos.

Chiropractors are uniquely positioned to spearhead this next evolution in structural and physical healing. As we have done many times before. The stage is set. Emotional and chemical practices and understanding have seen radical improvements to combat the onslaught of modern stressors. Now it is up to us, the physical practitioners, to give those something to anchor to. A nervous system to hold and guide them. Our profession now holds the keys to a future that our predecessors could only dream of. Yet in order to use those keys, we must first acknowledge that our old keys won't open that door. No matter how many fancy keyrings and positive intentions you imbue them with.

This is the final reframing I offer you: healing is not linear. It is cyclical. Spiralling. Seasonal. In this, Dr. Mark Postles and his model 'The Journey' is incredibly accurate. We ebb and flow through periods of symptoms, only to shoot out and up to a radically improved state of function and being. From there, our body stabilises and normalises the changes, resetting its neuromuscular frameworks and standards. Once this state of improvement is integrated and the body is ready, we repeat the process by dropping into the next symptomatic state. The next layer of the onion, the next barrier to be deconstructed. Each glimpse of the goal, the horizon, reorients the compass. Each correction makes return more possible. Each return strengthens the pathway until it becomes a dwelling place rather than a destination.

- The process played out over days changes weeks.

- The process played out over weeks changes months.

- The process played out over months changes years.

- The process played out over years changes generations.

- The process played out over generations changes the world.

- It is not an ascent toward perfection, but into integrity and resilience.

This book was never about answers. It is about re-examining the philosophy of our work. It is about the language of the field, and the field itself. The place beneath balance where healing is no longer elusive, but inevitable. Not because the work is done, but because, finally, it can begin. And when it does, it will not be as 'striving' or as 'fixing', but as reinhabiting the sacred intelligence of structure and soul. This is coherence. This is the continuum.

Renowned philosopher and poet David Whyte wrote in his book *Constellations:* 'No matter the self-conceited importance of our labours, we are all compost for worlds we cannot yet imagine'. So, may this work and these words make good compost for the future.

Yours in health,
Dr. Regan Osborne.

References

- Centeno, C. J., Schultz, J. R., Cheever, M., Robinson, B., Freeman, M. & Marinaro, K.M. (2014). Safety and complications reporting on the re-implantation of culture-expanded mesenchymal stem cells using autologous platelet lysate technique. *Clinical Medicine Insights: Arthritis and Musculoskeletal Disorders, 7*, 19–27.

- Center for Health Advocacy & Wellness (2025). *Managing stress.* https://chaw.fsu.edu/topics/wellness/managing-stress

- Haavik, H. & Murphy, B. A. (2012). The role of spinal manipulation in addressing disordered sensorimotor integration and altered motor control. *Journal of Electromyography and Kinesiology, 22*(5), 768–776.

- Hodges, P. W. & Richardson, C. A. (1996). Inefficient muscular stabilization of the lumbar spine associated with low back pain: A motor control evaluation of transversus abdominis. *Spine, 21*(22), 2640–2650.

- Hurrell, J. J. & Egli, R. (2010). Stress management in the workplace: Interventions and outcomes. *Occupational Medicine, 60*(1), 20–25.

- LeDoux, J. E. (2003). The emotional brain, fear, and the amygdala. *Cellular and Molecular Neurobiology, 23*(4–5), 727–738.

- Lelic, D., Niazi, I. K., Holt, K., Jochumsen, M., Dremstrup, K., Yielder, P., Murphy, B. & Haavik, H. (2016). Manipulation of dysfunctional spinal joints affects sensorimotor integration in the prefrontal cortex: A brain source localization study. *Neural Plasticity, 2016*, 3704964.

- Levine, P. A. and Frederick, A. (1997). *Waking the Tiger: Healing Trauma: The Innate Capacity to Transform Overwhelming Experiences*. North Atlantic Books.

- Lieberman, M. D., Eisenberger, N. I., Crockett, M. J., Tom, S. M., Pfeifer, J. H. & Way, B. M. (2007). Putting feelings into words: Affect labeling disrupts amygdala activity in response to affective stimuli. *Psychological Science, 18*(5), 421–428.

- McEwen, B. S. & Wingfield, J. C., (2003). The concept of allostasis in biology and biomedicine. *Hormones and Behavior, 43*(1), 2–15.

- Mitchell, T., O'Sullivan, P. B., Burnett, A. F., Straker, L. & Rudd, C. (2012). Identification of modifiable personal factors that predict new-onset low back pain: A prospective study of female nursing students. *Clinical Journal of Pain, 28*(6), 467–474.

- Monroe, S. M. & Simons, A. D., (1991). Diathesis–stress theories in the context of life stress research: Implications for the depressive disorders. *Psychological Bulletin, 110*(3), 406–425.

- New Zealand Chiropractors' Association, 2025. *Vertebral subluxation.* https://nzchiropractors.org/about-chiropractic/vertebral-subluxation/

- O'Keefe, J. H., Vogel, R., Lavie, C. J. & Cordain, L. (2012). Exercise like a hunter-gatherer: A prescription for organic fitness. *Progress in Cardiovascular Diseases, 55*(1), 16–26.

- Oxford English Dictionary (2025). *Trauma.* https://www.oed.com/dictionary/trauma_n

- Porges, S. W. (2011). *The Polyvagal Theory: Neurophysiological Foundations of Emotions, Attachment, Communication, and Self-Regulation.* W.W. Norton & Company.

- Proske, U. & Gandevia, S. C. (2012). The proprioceptive senses: Their roles in signalling body shape, body position and movement, and muscle force. *Physiological Reviews, 92*(4), 1651–1697.

- Roche, N., Lackmy, A., Achache, V., Bussel, B. & Katz, R. (2012). Effects of repetitive transcranial magnetic stimulation on normal and spastic stretch reflexes in humans. *Experimental Brain Research, 223*(3), 361–369.

- Sapolsky, R. M. (2004). *Why Zebras Don't Get Ulcers: The Acclaimed Guide to Stress, Stress-Related Diseases, and Coping* (3rd ed.).W.H. Freeman.

- Sterling, P. & Eyer, J. (1988). Allostasis: A new paradigm to explain arousal pathology. In Fisher, S. & Reason, J. (Eds.), *Handbook of Life Stress, Cognition and Health* (pp. 629–649). Wiley.

- Westcott, W. L. (2012). Resistance training is medicine: Effects of strength training on health. *Current Sports Medicine Reports, 11*(4), 209–216.